ESSAYS ON MODERN NOVELISTS

ESSAYS

ON

MODERN NOVELISTS

BY

WILLIAM LYON PHELPS

M.A. (HARVARD), PH.D. (YALE)

FORMERLY INSTRUCTOR IN ENGLISH AT HARVARD
LAMPSON PROFESSOR OF ENGLISH LITERATURE AT YALE

NEW YORK
THE BOOK LEAGUE OF AMERICA
1929

To My Wife

PREFACE

SOME of the essays in this volume have appeared in recent numbers of various periodicals. The essays on " Mark Twain " and " Thomas Hardy " were originally printed in the *North American Review;* those on " Mrs. Ward " and " Rudyard Kipling," in the *Forum;* those on "Alfred Ollivant," " Björnstjerne Björnson," and " Novels as a University Study," in the *Independent.* The same magazine contained a portion of the present essay on " Lorna Doone," while the article on " The Teacher's Attitude toward Contemporary Literature " was written for the *Chicago Interior.* My friend, Mr. Andrew Keogh, Reference Librarian of Yale University, has been kind enough to prepare the List of Publications, thereby increasing my debt to him for many previous favours.

W. L. P.

YALE UNIVERSITY,
Tuesday, 5 *October*, 1909.

CONTENTS

ESSAYS ON MODERN NOVELISTS

I

WILLIAM DE MORGAN

"How can you know whether you are successful or not at forty-one? How do you know you won't have a tremendous success, all of a sudden? Yes — after another ten years, perhaps — but *some* time! And then twenty years of real, happy work. It has all been before, this sort of thing. Why not you?" Thus spoke the hopeful Alice to the despairing Charley; and it makes an interesting comment on the very man who wrote the conversation, and created the speakers. It has indeed "all been before, this sort of thing"; only when an extremely clever person, whose friends have always been saying, with an exclamation rather than an interrogation point appended, "Why don't you write a novel!" . . . waits until he has passed his grand climacteric, he displays more faith in Providence than in himself. All of which is as it should be. Keats died at the age of twenty-five, but, from where I am now writing, I can reach his Poetical Works almost without leaving my chair; he is among the English Poets. Had Mr. De Morgan died at the age of twenty-five? The answer is, he didn't. I am no great believer in mute, inglorious Miltons, nor do I think that I daily pass potential novelists in the street. Life is shorter than Art, as has frequently been observed; but it seems long enough for Genius. Genius resembles murder in that it *will* out; you can no more prevent its expression than you can prevent the thrush from singing his song twice over. Crabbed age and youth have their peculiar accent. Keats, with all his glory, could not have written *Joseph Vance*, and Mr. De Morgan, with all his skill in ceramics, could not have fashioned the *Ode on a Grecian Urn.*

Sir Thomas Browne, who loved miracles, did not hesitate to classify the supposed importance of the grand climacteric as a vulgar error; he included a whole quaint chapter on the subject, in that old curiosity shop of literature, the *Pseudodoxia Epidemica.* "And so perhaps hath it happened unto the number 7. and 9. which multiplyed into themselves doe make up 63. commonly esteemed the great Climactericall of our lives; for the dayes of men are usually cast up by septenaries, and every seventh yeare conceived to carry some altering character with it, either in the temper of body, minde,

or both; but among all other, three are most remarkable, that is, 7. times 7. or forty-nine, 9. times 9.
or eighty-one, and 7. times 9. or the yeare of sixty-
three; which is conceived to carry with it, the most
considerable fatality, and consisting of both the
other numbers was apprehended to comprise the
vertue of either, is therefore expected and entertained with feare, and esteemed a favour of fate to
pass it over; which notwithstanding many suspect
but to be a Panick terrour, and men to feare they
justly know not what; and for my owne part, to
speak indifferently, I find no satisfaction, nor any
sufficiency in the received grounds to establish a
rationall feare."

Among various strong reasons against this super-
stition, Dr. Browne presents the impressive argument
shown by the Patriarchs: "the lives of our fore-
fathers presently after the flood, and more especially
before it, who, attaining unto 8. or 900. yeares, had
not their Climacters computable by digits, or as we
doe account them; for the great Climactericall was
past unto them before they begat children, or gave
any Testimony of their virilitie, for we read not that
any begat children before the age of sixtie five."

The strange case of William De Morgan would
have deeply interested Sir Thomas, and he would
have given it both full and minute consideration.
For it was just after he had safely passed the cli-

macterical year of sixty-three, that our now famous novelist began what is to us the most important chapter of his life, the first chapter of *Joseph Vance;* and, like the Patriarchs, it was only after he had reached the age of sixty-five that he became fruitful, producing those wonderful children of his brain that are to-day everywhere known and loved. Poets ripen early; if a man comes to his twenty-fifth birthday without having written some things supremely well, he may in most instances abandon all hope of immortality in song; but to every would-be novelist it is reasonable to whisper those encouraging words, "while there's life there's hope." Of the ten writers who may be classed as the greatest English novelists, only one — Charles Dickens — published a good novel before the age of thirty. Defoe's first fiction of any consequence was *Robinson Crusoe*, printed in 1719; he was then fifty-eight years old. Richardson had turned fifty before his earliest novel appeared. And although I can think at this moment of no case exactly comparable with that of the author of *Joseph Vance*, it is a book to which experience has contributed as well as inspiration, and would be something, if not inferior, at all events very different, had it been composed in early or in middle life. For it vibrates with the echoes of a long gallery, whose walls are crowded with interesting pictures.

WILLIAM DE MORGAN

The recent Romantic Revival has produced many novels that have enjoyed a brief and noisy popularity; its worst effects are noticeable on the minds of readers, unduly stimulated by the constant perusal of rapid-fire fiction. Many will not read further than the fourth page, unless some casualties have already occurred. To every writer who starts with some deliberation, they shout, "Leave your damnable faces and begin." Authors who produce for immediate consumption are prepared for this; so are the more clever men who write the publishers' advertisements. An announcement of a new work by an exceedingly fashionable novelist was headed by the appetising line, "This book goes with a rush, and ends with a smash." That would hardly do as a description of *Clarissa Harlowe*, *Wilhelm Meister*, or some other classics. To a highly nervous and irritably impatient reading public, a man whose name had no commercial value in literature gravely offered in the year of grace 1906 an "ill-written autobiography" of two hundred and eighty thousand words! Well, the result is what might *not* have been expected. If ever a confirmed optimist had reason to feel justification of his faith, Mr. De Morgan must have seen it in the reception given to his first novel.

Despite the great length of Mr. De Morgan's books, and the leisurely passages of comment and

rather extraneous detail, he never *begins* slowly.
No producer of ephemeral trash, no sensation-
monger, has ever got under way with more speed,
or taken a swifter initial plunge into the very heart
of action. One memorable day in 1873, Count
Tolstoi picked up a little story by Pushkin, which
his ten-year-old son had been reading aloud to a
member of the family. The great Russian glanced
at the first sentence, "The guests began to assemble
the evening before the *fête*." He was mightily
pleased. "That's the way to begin a story!" he
cried. "The reader is taken by one stroke into
the midst of the action. Another writer would have
commenced by describing the guests, the rooms,
while Pushkin — he goes straight at his goal."
Some of those in the room laughed, and suggested
that Tolstoi himself appropriate such a beginning
and write a novel. He immediately retired and
wrote the first sentences of *Anna Karenina;* which
is literally the manner in which that masterpiece
came into being.[1] Now if one will open any of Mr.
De Morgan's works, he will find the procedure that
Tolstoi praised. Something immediately happens —
happens before we have any idea of the real character of the agents, and before we hardly know where
we are. Indeed, the first chapter of *Somehow Good*

[1] *Léon Tolstoi: Vie et Œuvres. Mémoires par P. Birukov.
Traduction Française,* Tome III, p. 177.

may serve as an artistic model for the commence-
ment of a novel. It is written with extraordinary
vivacity and spirit. But the author understands
better how to begin his works than he does how to
end them. The close of *Joseph Vance* is like the
mouth of the Mississippi, running off into the open
sea through a great variety of passages. The ending of *Alice-for-Short* is accomplished only by notes,
comment, and citations. And *Somehow Good* is simply snipped off, when it might conceivably have proceeded on its way. His fourth novel is the only one
that ends as well as it begins.

You cannot judge books, any more than you can
individuals, by the first words they say. If I could
only discover somewhere some man, woman, or child
who had not read *Joseph Vance*, I should like to
tell him the substance of the first chapter, and ask
him to guess what sort of a story had awakened my
enthusiasm. Suppose some person who had never
heard of Browning should stumble on *Pauline*, and
read the first three lines : —

"Pauline, mine own, bend o'er me — thy soft breast
Shall pant to mine — bend o'er me — thy sweet eyes,
And loosened hair and breathing lips, and arms"

one sees the sharp look of expectation on the reader's
face, and one almost laughs aloud to think what
there is in store for him. He will very soon exhibit

symptoms of bewilderment, and before he has finished the second page he will push the book aside with an air of pious disappointment. No slum story ever opened more promisingly than *Joseph Vance*. We are led at the very start into a dirty rum-shop; there immediately ensues a fight between two half-drunken loafers in the darkness without; this results in the double necessity of the police and the hospital; and a broken bottle, found against a dead cat, is the missile employed to destroy a human eye. In *Alice-for-Short*, the first chapter shows us a ragged little girl of six carrying a jug of beer from a public-house to a foul basement, where dwell her father and mother, both victims of alcohol. The police again. On the third page of *Somehow Good*, we have the "fortune to strike on a rich vein of so-called life in a London slum." The hero gives a drunken, murderous scoundrel a "blow like the kick of a horse, that lands fairly on the eye socket with a cracking concussion that can be heard above the tumult, and is followed by a roar of delight from the male vermin." Once more the police. *It Never can Happen Again* begins in a corner of London unspeakably vile.

Zola and Gorky at their best, and worst — for it is sometimes hard to make the distinction — have not often surpassed the first chapters of Mr. De Morgan's four novels. Never has a writer waded more unflinchingly into the slime. And yet the very last word to characterise these books would be the word "slum-stories." The foundations of Mr. De Morgan's work, like the foundations of cathedrals, are deep in the dirt; but the total impression is one of exceeding beauty. Indeed, with our novelist's conception of life, as a progress toward something high and sublime, where evil not only exists, but is a necessary factor in development, the darkness of the shadows proves the intense radiance of the sun. The planet Venus is so bright, we are accustomed to remark, that it sometimes casts a shadow. Christopher Vance emerges from beastly degradation to a position of power, influence, and usefulness; the Heath family, in receiving Alice, entertain an angel unawares; and the march of *Somehow Good* goes from hell, through purgatory, and into paradise. It is a divine comedy, in more ways than one; and shows that sometimes the goal of ill is very unlike the start.

We had not read far into *Joseph Vance* before we shouted *Dickens Redivivus!* or some equivalent remark in the vernacular. We made this outcry with no tincture of depreciation and with no yelp of the plagiarism-hunting hound. It requires little skill to observe the similarity to Dickens, as was proved by the fact that everyone noticed it. In general, the shout was one of glad recognition; it was the welcome given to the sound of a voice that had been still. It was not an imitation: it was a reincarnation. The spirit of Dickens had really entered into William De Morgan; many chapters in *Joseph Vance* sounded as if they had been dictated by the ghost of the author of *Copperfield*. No book since 1870 had given so vivid an impression of the best-beloved of all English novelists. This is meant to be high praise. When Walt Whitman was being exalted for his unlikeness to the great poets, one sensible critic quietly remarked, "It is easier to differ from the great poets than to resemble them." To "remind us of Dickens" would be as difficult for many modern novelists as for a molehill to remind us of the Matterhorn.

We may say, however, that *Joseph Vance* and *It Never can Happen Again* are more like Dickens in character and in detail than is *Alice-for-Short;* and that the latter is closer to Dickens than is *Somehow Good*. The Reverend Benaiah Capstick infallibly calls to mind the spiritual adviser of Mrs. Weller; with the exception that the latter was also spirituous. That kind of religion does not seem strongly to appeal to either novelist; for Mr. Stiggins took to drink, and Capstick to an insane asylum. There are many things in the conversation of Christopher Vance that recall the humorous world-wisdom of the elder Weller; and so we might

continue, were it profitable. Another great point
of resemblance between Mr. De Morgan and
Dickens is seen in the method of narration chosen
by each. Here William De Morgan is simply following in the main track of English fiction, where the
novelist cannot refrain from *editing* the text of the
story. The course of events is constantly interrupted by the author's gloss. Now when the
author's mind is not particularly interesting, the
comment is an unpleasant interruption; it is both
impertinent and dull. But when the writer is himself more profound, more clever, and more entertaining than even his best characters, we cannot
have too much of him. It is true that Mr. De
Morgan has told a good story in each of his novels;
but it is also true that the story is not the cause
of their reputation. We read these books with delight
because the characters are so attractive, and because
the author's comments on them and on events are
so penetrating. If it is true, as some have intimated,
that this method of novel-writing proves that Mr.
De Morgan, whatever he is, is not a literary artist,
then it is undeniable that Fielding, Dickens, Trollope,
and Thackeray are not artists; which is absurd,
as Euclid would say. Great books are invariably
greater than our definitions of them. Browning
and Wagner composed great works of Art without
paying much attention to the rules of the game.

As compared with French and Russian fiction, English novels from Fielding to De Morgan have unquestionably sounded a note of insincerity. One reason for this lies in the fact that to the Anglo-Saxon mind, Morality has always seemed infinitely more important than Art. Matthew Arnold spent his life fighting the Philistines; but when he said that conduct was three-fourths of life, there was jubilation in the enemy's camp. Now Zola declared that a novel could no more be called immoral in its descriptions than a text-book on physiology; the novelist commits a sin when he writes a badly constructed sentence. A disciple of this school insisted that it was more important to have an accurate sense of colour than to have a clear notion of right and wrong. Fortunately for the true greatness of humanity, you never can get the average Englishman or American to swallow such doctrine. But it is at the same time certain that among English-speaking peoples Art has seldom been taken with sufficient seriousness. We are handy with our fists; but you cannot imagine us using them in behalf of literature, as we do for real or personal property. So far as I know, an English audience in the theatre has never been excited on a purely artistic question — a matter of frequent occurrence on the Continent. We seem to believe that, after all, Art has no place in the serious business of life; it is a recreation, to

amuse a mind overstrained by money-making or
by political affairs. We leave it to women, who are
supposed to have more leisure for trifles.

For this reason, English novelists have generally
felt compelled to treat their public as a tired mother
treats a restless child. Our novelists have been in
mortal terror lest the attention of their audience
should wander; and instead of taking their work
and their readers seriously, they continually hand
us lollipops. Their attitude is at once apologetic
and insulting. They do not dare to believe that a
great work of Art — without personal comment —
has in itself moral greatness, and they do not dare
trust the intelligence of spectators, but must forsooth
constantly break the illusion by soothing or ex-
planatory remarks. The fact that in our greatest
writers this is often presented from the standpoint
of humour, does not prevent the loss of illusion; and
in writers who are not great, the reader feels nothing
but indignation. In the first chapter of the third
book of *Amelia*, we find the following advice: —

"He then proceeded as Miss Matthews desired; but, lest
all our readers should not be of her opinion, we will, according
to our usual custom, endeavour to accommodate ourselves to
every taste, and shall, therefore, place this scene in a chapter
by itself, which we desire all our readers who do not love, or
who, perhaps, do not know the pleasure of tenderness, to pass
over; since they may do this without any prejudice to the
thread of the narrative."

In the first chapter of *Shirley*, Charlotte Brontë prologises as follows : —

"If you think . . . that anything like a romance is preparing for you, reader, you never were more mistaken. . . . Calm your expectations; reduce them to a lowly standard. Something real, cool, and solid lies before you; . . . It is not positively affirmed that you shall not have a taste of the exciting, perhaps toward the middle and close of the meal, but it is resolved that the first dish set upon the table shall be one that a Catholic — ay, even an Anglo-Catholic — might eat on Good Friday in Passion Week; it shall be cold lentils and vinegar without oil; it shall be unleavened bread with bitter herbs, and no roast lamb."

William Black once wrote a novel called *Madcap Violet*, which he intended for a tragedy, and in which, therefore, we have a right to expect some artistic dignity. About midway in the volume we find the following : —

"At this point, and in common courtesy to his readers, the writer of these pages considers himself bound to give fair warning that the following chapter deals solely and wholly with the shooting of mergansers, curlews, herons, and such like fearful wild fowl; therefore, those who regard such graceless idling with aversion, and are anxious to get on with the story, should at once proceed to chapter twenty-three."

At the beginning of the second chapter of *Dr. Thorne*, one of the best of Trollope's novels, we are petted in this manner : —

WILLIAM DE MORGAN

"A few words must still be said about Miss Mary before we rush into our story; the crust will then have been broken, and the pie will be open to the guests."

At the three hundred and seventy-second page of the late Marion Crawford's entertaining story, *The Prima Donna,* the course of the narrative is thus interrupted: —

"Now at this stage of my story it would be unpardonable to keep my readers in suspense, if I may suppose that any of them have a little curiosity left. Therefore, I shall not narrate in detail what happened Friday, Saturday, and Sunday, seeing that it was just what might have been expected to happen at a week-end party during the season when there is nothing in the world to do but to play golf, tennis, or croquet, or to write or drive all day, and to work hard at bridge all the evening; for that is what it has come to."

Finally, in the first chapter of Mr. Winston Churchill's novel, *Coniston,* the author pleads with his reader in this style: —

"The reader is warned that this first love-story will, in a few chapters, come to an end; and not to a happy end — otherwise there would be no book. Lest he should throw the book away when he arrives at this page, it is only fair to tell him that there is another and much longer love-story later on, if he will only continue to read, in which, it is hoped, he may not be disappointed."

Imagine Turgenev or Flaubert scribbling anything similar to the interpolations quoted above! When a great French novelist does condescend to speak to his reader, it is in a tone, that so far from belittling his own art, or sugaring the expectation of his listener, has quite the contrary effect. On the second page of *Père Goriot,* we find the following solemn warning: —

"Ainsi ferez-vous, vous qui tenez ce livre d'une main blanche, vous qui vous enfoncez dans un moïleux fauteuil en vous disant: 'Peut-être ceci va-t-il m'amuser.' Après avoir lu les secrètes infortunes du père Goriot, vous dînerez avec appétit en mettant votre insensibilité sur le compte de l'auteur, en le taxant d'exagération, en l'accusant de poésie. Ah! sachez-le: ce drame n'est ni une fiction ni un roman. *All is true,* il est si véritable, que chacun peut en reconnaître les éléments chez soi, dans son cœur peut-être."

The chief objection to these constant remarks to the reader, so common in great English novels, is that they for the moment destroy the illusion. Suppose an actress in the midst of Ophelia's mad scene should suddenly pause and address the audience in her own accents in this wise: "I observe that some ladies among the spectators are weeping, and that some men are yawning. Allow me to say to those of you who dislike tragic events on the stage, that I shall remain here only a few moments longer, and shall not have much to say; and that if you will only be patient, the grave-diggers will come on before long, and it is probable that their conversation will amuse you."

The two reasons given above, the fear that a novel unexplained by author's comment will not justify itself morally, and that at all hazards the gentle reader must be placated and entertained, undoubtedly partly explain a long tradition in the course of English fiction. But while we may protest against this sort of thing in general, it is well to remember that we must take our men of genius as we find them, and rejoice that they have seen fit to employ any channel of expression. There are many different kinds of great novels, as there are of great poems. The fact that Tennyson's poetry belongs to the first class does not in the least prevent the totally different poetry of Browning from being ranked equally high. *Joseph Vance* is a very different kind of novel from *The Return of the Native*, but both awaken our wonder and delight. There are some books that inspire us by their art, and there are others that inspire us by their ideas. Turgenev was surely a greater artist than Tolstoi, but *Anna Karenina* is a veritable piece of life.

I do not say that William De Morgan is not a great artist, because, if I should say it, I should not know exactly what I meant. But the immense pleasure that his books give me is another kind of pleasure than I receive from *The Scarlet Letter*. *Joseph Vance* is not so much a beautifully written or exquisitely constructed novel as it is an encyclopædia of life. We meet real people, we hear delightful conversation, and the tremendously interesting personality of the author is everywhere apparent. The opinion of many authors concerning immortality is not worth attention; but I should very much like to know Mr. De Morgan's views on this absorbing subject. And so I turn to the fortieth chapter of *Joseph Vance* with great expectations. The reader is advised to skip this chapter, a sure indication of its importance. For, like all humorists, Mr. De Morgan is a bit shamefaced when he talks about the deepest things, the things that really interest him most. It surely will not do to have Dr. Thorpe talk like the Reverend Mr. Capstick, although they both eagerly discuss what we call the supernatural. Capstick is an ass, but he has one characteristic that we might, to a certain extent, imitate; he sees no reason to apologise for conversing on great topics, or to break up such a conversation with an embarrassed laugh. Most of us are horribly afraid of being taken for sanctimonious persons, when there is really not the slightest danger. We are always pleasantly surprised when we discover that our friends are at heart just as serious as we are, and that they, too, regret the mask of flippancy that our Anglo-Saxon false modesty compels us to wear. But, as some one has said, you cannot expect your audience to take your views seriously unless you express them with seriousness. Mr. De Morgan, like Robert Browning, would doubtless deny that Dr. Thorpe spoke only the author's thoughts; but just as you can hear Browning's voice all through those "utterances of so many imaginary persons, not mine," so I feel confident that amid all the light banter of this charming talk in the fortieth chapter, the following remark of Dr. Thorpe expresses the philosophy of William De Morgan, and at the same time the basal moral principle underlying this entire novel: — "The highest good is the growth of the Soul, and the greatest man is he who rejoices most in great fulfilments of the will of God."

For although Mr. De Morgan belongs, like Dickens, to the great humorists, who, while keenly conscious of the enormous difference between right and wrong, regard the world with a kindly smile for human weakness and folly, he is mainly a psychologist. To all of his novels he might appropriately have prefixed the words of the author of *Sordello:* "My stress lay on the incidents in the development of a soul; little else is worth study." All the characters that he loves show *soul-development;* the few characters that are unlovely have souls that do not advance. Joseph, Lossie, Janey, Alicia, Charles Heath, Rosalind, Athelstan, have the inner man renewed day by day; one feels that at physical death such personalities proceed naturally into a sphere of eternal progress. On the other hand, Joey's soul stands still; so do the souls of Violet, Lavinia Straker, Mrs. Vereker, Mrs. Eldridge, Judith, and Mrs. Craik. Why should they live for ever? They would always be the same. This is the real distinction in these novels between people that are fundamentally good and those that are fundamentally bad; whether their badness causes tragedy or merely constant irritation. It is an original manner of dividing virtue from vice, but it is illuminating.

The events in Mr. De Morgan's books are improbable, but the people are probable. The same might be said of Shakespeare. It is highly improbable that Christopher Vance could have risen to fortune through his sign-board, or that Fenwick should have been electrocuted at the feet of his wife's daughter. But Christopher Vance, Fenwick, and Sally behave precisely as people would behave in such emergencies in real life. In many ways I think Christopher Vance is the most convincing character in all the novels; at any rate, I had rather hear him talk than any of the others. There is no trace of meanness in him, and even when he is drunk he is never offensive or disgusting. The day after he has returned intoxicated from a meeting of the Board of Arbitrators, he seems rather inquisitive as to his exact condition, and asks his son: —

"I wasn't singin' though, Nipper, was I?" I said certainly not! "Not 'a Landlady of France she loved an
Officer, 'tis said,' nor 'stick 'em up again in the middle of
a three-cent pie'?"

"Neither of them — quite certain." My father seemed
reassured. "That's *something*, anyhow," said he. "The
other Arbitrators was singin' both. Likewise 'Rule Britan-
nia.' Weak-headed cards, the two on 'em!"

The scene at Christopher Vance's death-bed, when
Joseph finally discloses the identity of the boy who
threw the piece of glass into the eye of the Sweep,
touches the depths of true pathos. One feels the
infinite love of the father for the little son who defended him. He is quite rightly prouder of that
exploit than of all the Nipper's subsequent learning.

While the imaginary events in this novel bear no
sort of relation to the circumstances of the author's
own life, I cannot help launching the mere guess that
the father of William De Morgan was, to a certain
extent, a combination of Christopher Vance and Dr.
Thorpe. For Augustus De Morgan was not only
a distinguished mathematical scholar, he was well-
known for the keenness of his wit. He had the
learning and refinement of Dr. Thorpe, and the
shrewd, irresistible humour of old Vance. At all
events, this striking combination in the novelist
can be traced to no more probable source.

The influence of good women on men's lives is
repeatedly shown; it is indeed a leading principle

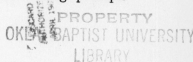

in three of the books. One of the most notable differences in novels that reflect a pessimistic *Weltanschauung* from those that indicate the contrary may be seen right here. How completely the whole significance of the works of Guy de Maupassant would change had he included here and there some women who combined virtue with personal charm! "Were there no women, men would live like gods," said a character in one of Dekker's plays; judged by much modern fiction, one would feel like trying the experiment. But what would become of Mr. De Morgan's novels, and of the attitude toward life they so clearly reflect, if they contained no women? Young Joseph Vance was fortunate indeed in having in his life the powerful influence of two such characters as Lossie Thorpe and Janey Spencer. They were what a compass is to a shipman, taking him straight on his course through the blackest storms. It was for Lossie that he made the greatest sacrifice in his whole existence; and nothing pays a higher rate of moral interest than a big sacrifice. It was Janey who led him from the grossness of earth into the spiritual world, something that Lossie, with all her loveliness, could not do. Both women show that there is nothing inherently dull in goodness; it may be accompanied with some *esprit*. We are too apt to think that moral goodness is represented by such persons as the Elder Brother in the story of the Prodigal Son, when the parable indicates that the younger brother, with all his crimes, was actually the more virtuous of the two. It took no small skill for Mr. De Morgan to create such an irresistibly good woman as Lossie, make his hero in love with her from boyhood, cause her to marry some one else, and then to unite the heart-broken hero with another girl; and through these tremendous upheavals to make all things work together for good, and to the reader's complete satisfaction. This could not possibly have been accomplished had not the author been able to fashion a woman, who, while totally unlike Lossie in every physical and mental aspect, was spiritually even more attractive. I am not sure which of the two girls has the bigger place in their maker's heart; I suspect it is Lossie; but to me Janey is not only a better woman, I really have a stronger affection for her.

In *Alice-for-Short*, the hero is again blessed with two guardian angels, his sister and his second wife. Mr. De Morgan is extremely generous to his favourite men, in permitting either their second choice or their second experiment in matrimony to prove such an amazing success. Comparatively few novelists dare to handle the problem of happy second marriages; the subject for some reason does not lend itself readily to romance. Josh Billings said he knew of absolutely nothing that would cure a man of laziness; but that a second wife would sometimes help. Although he said this in the spirit of farce, it is exactly what happens in Mr. De Morgan's books. Janey is not technically a second wife, but she is spiritually; and she rescues Joseph from despair, restores his ambition and capacity to work, and after her death is like a guiding star. Alice is a second wife, both in her husband's heart and in the law; and her influence on Charles Heath provides exactly the stimulus needed to save him from himself. Fenwick marries for the second time, and although his wife is in one sense the same person, in another she is not; she is quite different in everything except constancy from the wretched girl he left sobbing on the verandah in India. And what would have become of Fenwick without the mature Rosalind? Salvation, in Mr. De Morgan's novels, often assumes a feminine shape. They are not books of Friendship, like *The Cloister and the Hearth*, *Trilby*, and *Es War;* with all their wonderful intelligence and play of intellect, they would seem almost barren without women. And he is far more successful in depicting love after marriage than before. One of the most charming characteristics of these stories is the frequent representation of the highest happiness known on earth — not found in the passion of early youth, but in a union of two hearts cemented

by joy and sorrow in the experience of years. No
novelist has ever given us better pictures of a good
English home; more attractive glimpses into the
reserveless intimacy of the affairs of the hearth.
The conversations between Christopher Vance and
his wife, between Sir Rupert and Lady Johnson,
between Fenwick and Rosalind, are decidedly superior to the "love-making" scenes. Indeed, the
description of the walk during which young Dr.
Vereker definitely wins Sally, is disappointing.
It is perhaps the only important episode in Mr.
De Morgan's novels that shows more effort than
inspiration.

The style in these books, despite constant quota-
tion, is not at all a literary style. Joseph Vance
is called "an ill-written autobiography," because
it lacks entirely the conventional manner. Many
works of fiction are composed in what might be called
the terminology of the art; just as works in science
and in sport are compelled to repeat constantly the
same verbal forms. The astonishing freshness
and charm of Mr. De Morgan's method consist
partly in his abandonment of literary precedent,
and adhering only to actual observation. It is as
though an actor on the stage should suddenly drop
his mannerism of accent and gesture, and behave
as he would were he actually, instead of histrionically,
happy or wretched. Despite the likeness to Dickens

in characters and atmosphere, *Joseph Vance* sounds
not only as though its author had never written a
novel previously, but as though he had never read
one. It has the strangeness of reality. There is
no lack of action in these huge narratives: the men
and women pass through the most thrilling incidents,
and suffer the greatest extremes of passion, pain,
and joy that the human mind can endure. We have
three cases of drowning, one tremendous fire; and
in *Somehow Good* — which, viewed merely as a
story, is the best of them — a highly eventful plot;
and, spiritually, the characters give us an idea of
how much agony the heart can endure without quite
breaking. But though the bare plot seems almost
like melodrama, the style is never on stilts. In the
most awful crises, the language has the absolute
simplicity of actual circumstance. When Rosalind
recognises her husband in the cab, we wonder why
she takes it so coolly. Some sixty pages farther
along, we come upon this paragraph: —

"Nevertheless, these were not so absolute that her de-
meanour escaped comment from the cabby, the only witness
of her first sight of the 'electrocuted' man. He spoke of her
afterwards as that squealing party down that sanguinary
little turning off Shepherd's Bush Road he took that sanguinary galvanic shock to."

Our author is fond of presenting events of the most
momentous consequence through the lips of humble

and indifferent observers. It is only the cabman's chance testimony which shows us that even Rosalind's superb self-control had the limit determined by real womanhood; and in *Joseph Vance*, the great climax of emotion, when Lossie visits her maligned old lover, is given with unconscious force through the faulty vernacular of the "slut" of a servant-maid, who is utterly unaware of the angels that ministered over that scene; and then by the broken English of the German chess-player, equally blind to the divine presence. Compare these two crude testimonies, which make the ludicrous blunders made by the Hostess in that marvellous account of the death of Falstaff, and you have a veritable harmony of the Gospels. Some novelists use an extraordinary style to describe ordinary events; Mr. De Morgan uses an ordinary style to describe extraordinary events.

Even in his latest book, *It Never Can Happen Again*,[1] the least cheerful of all his productions, the title is intended to be as comforting as Charles Reade's caption, *It Is Never Too Late to Mend*. In this story, Mr. De Morgan descends into hell. Delirium tremens has never been pictured with more frightful horror than in the awful night when the mad wretch is bent on murder. No scene in any

---

[1] Through the kindness of Messrs. Henry Holt and Co., I have had the privilege of reading this novel in proof sheets.

naturalistic novel surpasses this in vivid detail.
Indeed, all of Mr. De Morgan's books might well
be circulated as anti-alcohol tracts; the real villain
in his tragedies is Drink. Even though drunkenness
in a certain aspect supplies comedy in *Joseph Vance*,
drink is, after all, the ruin of old Christopher, and we
are left with no shade of doubt that this is so. Mr.
De Morgan's unquestionable optimism does not
blink the dreadful aspects of life, any more than
did Browning's. The scene in the hospital, where
the fingers without finger-nails clasp the mighty
hand in the rubber glove, is as loathsomely horrible
as anything to be found in the annals of disease.
And the career of Blind Jim, entirely ignorant of
his divine origin and destiny, is a series of appalling
calamities. He has lost his sight in a terrible accident; he is run over by a waggon, and loses his
leg; he is run over by an automobile, and loses his
life. He has also lost, though he does not know it,
what is far dearer to him than eyes, or legs, or life,
— his little daughter. And yet we do not need
the spirit voice of the dead child to assure us that
all is well. Indeed, the tragic history of Jim and
Lizarann is not nearly so depressing as the humdrum narrative of the melancholy quarrel between
Mr. and Mrs. Challis. In previous novels, the author
has been pleased to show us domestic happiness;
here we have the dreary round of perpetual discord.

Of course no one can complain of Mr. De Morgan for his choice in this matter; it is certainly true that not all marriages are happy, even though the majority of them (as I believe) are. The difficulty is that the triangle in this book — husband, wife, and beautiful young lady — has no corner of real interest. It is not entirely the fault of either Mr. or Mrs. Challis that they separate; there is much to be said on both sides. What we object to is the fact that it is impossible to sympathise with either of them; this is not because each is guilty, but because neither is interesting. We do not much care what becomes of them. And as for Judith, the technical virgin who causes all the trouble, she is a very dull person. We do not need this book to learn that female beauty without brains fascinates the ordinary man. The best scenes are those where Blind Jim and Lizarann appear; they are a couple fully worthy of Dickens at his best. Unfortunately they do not appear often enough to suit us, and they both die. We could more easily have spared Mr. and Mrs. Challis, the latter's abominable tea-gossip friend, and that old hypocritical tiger-cat, Mrs. Challis's mother. Why does Mr. De Morgan make elderly women so disgustingly unattractive? Does his sympathy with life desert him here? The entire Challis household, including the satellites of relationship and propinquity, are hardly worth the author's

skill or the reader's attention. One would suppose
that a brilliant novelist, like Challis, pulled from the
domestic orbit by a comet like Judith, would be
for a time in an interesting, if not an edifying, position; but he is not. Perhaps Mr. De Morgan
wishes to show with the impartiality of a true
chronicler of life that a married man, drawn away
by his own lust, and enticed, can be just as dull in
sin as in virtue. Yet the long dreary family storm
ends in sunshine; the discordant pair are redeemed
by Love, — the real motive power of this story, —
and one feels that it can never happen again. In
spite of Mr. De Morgan's continual onslaught on
creeds, Athelstan Taylor, who believes the whole
Apostles' Creed, compares very favourably with
Challis, who believes only the first seven and the
last four words of it, apparently the portion accepted
by Mr. De Morgan: and by their fruits ye shall
know them. It is certainly a proof of the fair-
mindedness of our novelist, that he has created
orthodox believers like Lossie's husband and Athelstan Taylor, big wholesome fellows, both of them;
and has deliberately made both so irresistibly attractive. The professional parson is often ridiculed
in modern novels; it is worth noting that in this
story the only important character in the whole
work who combines intelligence with virtue is the
Reverend Athelstan Taylor.

Seldom have any books shown so intimate a knowledge of the kingdom of this world and at the same time reflected with such radiance the kingdom of heaven. It is noteworthy and encouraging that a man who portrays with such humorous exactitude the things that are seen and temporal, should exhibit so firm a faith in the things that are unseen and eternal. In *Joseph Vance* we have the growth of the soul from an environment of poverty and crime to the loftiest heights of nobility and self-denial; and the theme in the Waldstein Sonata triumphantly repeats the confidence of Dr. Thorpe, who regards death not as a barrier, but as a gateway. In *Alice-for-Short*, the mystery of the spirit-world completely envelops the humdrum inconsistencies that form the daily round, the trivial task; this is seen perhaps not so much in the "ghosts," for they speak of the past; but the figure of old Verrinder — whose heart revolves about the Asylum like the planet around the sun — and the waking of old Jane from her long sleep, seem to symbolise the impotence of Time to quench the divine spark of Love. This story is called a "dichronism"; but it might have been called a *dichroism*, for from one viewpoint it reflects only the clouded colour of earth, and from another a celestial glory. In *Somehow Good* the ugliest tragedy takes its place in the unapparent order of life. It is not that good finally reigns in spite of evil; the final truth is that in some manner good is the very goal of ill. The agony of separation has tested the pure metal of character; and the fusion of two lives is made permanent in the frightful heat of awful pain. The fruit of a repulsive sin may be Beauty, like a flower springing from a dung-hill. "What became of the baby? . . . *The* baby — *his* baby — *his* horrible baby!" "Gerry darling! Gerry *dearest!* do think . . ."

II

THOMAS HARDY

THE father of Thomas Hardy wished his son to enter the church, and this object was the remote goal of his early education. At just what period in the boy's mental development Christianity took on the form of a meaningless fable, we shall perhaps never know; but after a time he ceased to have even the faith of a grain of mustard seed. This absence of religious belief has proved no obstacle to many another candidate for the Christian ministry, as every habitual church-goer knows; or as any son of Belial may discover for himself by merely reading the prospectus of summer schools of theology. There has, however, always been a certain cold, mathematical precision in Mr. Hardy's way of thought that would have made him as uncomfortable in the pulpit as he would have been in an editor's chair, writing for salary persuasive articles containing the exact opposite of his individual convictions. But, although the beauty of holiness failed to impress his mind, the beauty of the sanctuary was sufficiently obvious to his sense of Art. He became an ecclesiastical architect, and for some years his delight was in the courts of the Lord. Instead of composing sermons in ink, he made sermons in stones, restoring to many a decaying edifice the outlines that the original builder had seen in his vision centuries ago. For no one has ever regarded ancient churches with more sympathy and reverence than Mr. Hardy. No man to-day has less respect for God and more devotion to His house.

Mr. Hardy's professional career as an architect extended over a period of about thirteen years, from the day when the seventeen-year-old boy became articled, to about 1870, when he forsook the pencil for the pen. His strict training as an architect has been of enormous service to him in the construction of his novels, for skill in constructive drawing has repeatedly proved its value in literature. Rossetti achieved positive greatness as an artist and as a poet. Stevenson's studies in engineering were not lost time, and Mr. De Morgan affords another good illustration of the same fact. Thackeray was unconsciously learning the art of the novelist while he was making caricatures, and the lesser Thackeray of a later day — George du Maurier — found the transition from one art to the other a natural progression. Hopkinson Smith and Frederic Remington, on a lower but dignified plane, bear witness to the same truth. Indeed, when one studies carefully the beginnings of the work of imaginative writers, one is surprised at the great number who have handled an artist's or a draughtsman's pencil. A prominent and successful playwright of to-day has said that if he were not writing plays, he should not dream of writing books; he would be building bridges.

Mr. Hardy's work as an ecclesiastical architect laid the real foundations of his success as a novelist; for it gave him an intimate familiarity with the old monuments and rural life of Wessex, and at the same time that eye for precision of form that is so noticeable in all his books. He has really never ceased to be an architect. Architecture has contributed largely to the matter and to the style of his stories. Two architects appear in his first novel. In *A Pair of Blue Eyes* Stephen Smith is a professional architect, and in coming to restore the old Western Church he was simply repeating the experience of his creator. No one of Mr. Hardy's novels contains more of the facts of his own life than *A Laodicean*, which was composed on what the author then believed to be his death-bed; it was mainly dictated, which I think partly accounts for its difference in style from the other tales. The hero, Somerset, is an architect whose first meeting with his future

wife occurs through his professional curiosity concerning the castle; and a considerable portion of
the early chapters is taken up with architectural
detail, and of his enforced rivalry with a competitor
in the scheme for restoration. Not only does Mr.
Hardy's scientific profession speak through the
mouths of his characters, but old and beautiful
buildings adorn his pages as they do the landscape
he loves. In *Two on a Tower* the ancient structure
appears here and there in the story as naturally and
incidentally as it would to a pedestrian in the neigh-
bourhood; in *A Pair of Blue Eyes* the church tower
plays an important part in a thrilling episode, and its
fall emphasises a Scripture text in a diabolical manner.
The old church at Weatherbury is so closely as-
sociated with the life history of the men and women
in *Far from the Madding Crowd* that as one stands
in front of it to-day the people seem to gather again
about its portal. . . .

But while Mr. Hardy has drawn freely on his
knowledge of architecture in furnishing animate
and inanimate material for his novels, the great
results of his youthful training are seen in a more
subtle and profounder influence. The intellectual
delight that we receive in the perusal of his books
— a delight that sometimes makes us impatient
with the work of feebler authors — comes largely
from the architectonics of his literary structures.

One never loses sight of Hardy the architect. In purely constructive skill he has surpassed all his contemporaries. His novels — with the exception of *Desperate Remedies* and *Jude the Obscure* — are as complete and as beautiful to contemplate as a sculptor's masterpiece. They are finished and noble works of art, and give the same kind of pleasure to the mind as any superbly perfect outline. Mr. Hardy himself firmly believes that the novel should first of all be a story: that it should not be a thesis, nor a collection of reminiscences or *obiter dicta*. He insists that a novel should be as much of a whole as a living organism, where all the parts — plot, dialogue, character, and scenery — should be fitly framed together, giving the single impression of a completely harmonious building. One simply cannot imagine him writing in the manner of a German novelist, with absolutely no sense of proportion; nor like the mighty Tolstoi, who steadily sacrifices Art on the altar of Reality; nor like the great English school represented by Thackeray, Dickens, Trollope, and De Morgan, whose charm consists in their intimacy with the reader; they will interrupt the narrative constantly to talk it over with the merest bystander, thus gaining his affection while destroying the illusion. Mr. Hardy's work shows a sad sincerity, the noble austerity of the true artist, who feels the dignity of his art and is quite willing to let it speak for itself.

His earliest novel, *Desperate Remedies*, is more like an architect's first crude sketch than a complete and detailed drawing. Strength, originality, and a thoroughly intelligent design are perfectly clear; one feels the impelling mind behind the product. But it resembles the *plan* of a good novel rather than a novel itself. The lines are hard; there is a curious rigidity about the movement of the plot which proceeds in jerks, like a machine that requires frequent winding up. The manuscript was submitted to a publishing firm, who, it is interesting to remember, handed it over to their professional reader, George Meredith. Mr. Meredith told the young author that his work was promising; and he said it in such a way that the two men became lifelong friends, there being no more jealousy between them than existed between Tennyson and Browning. Years later Mr. Meredith said that he regarded Mr. Hardy as the real leader of contemporary English novelists; and the younger man always maintained toward his literary adviser an attitude of sincere reverence, of which his poem on the octogenarian's death was a beautiful expression. There is something fine in the honest friendship and mutual admiration of two giants, who cordially recognise each other above the heads of the crowd, and who are themselves placidly unmoved by the fierce jealousy of their partisans. In this instance, despite a total unlikeness in literary style, there was genuine intellectual kinship. Mr. Meredith and Mr. Hardy were both Pagans and regarded the world and men and women from the Pagan standpoint, though the deduction in one case was optimism and in the other pessimism. Given the premises, the younger writer's conclusions seem more logical; and the processes of his mind were always more orderly than those of his brilliant and irregular senior. There is little doubt (I think) as to which of the two should rank higher in the history of English fiction, where fineness of Art surely counts for something. Mr. Hardy is a great novelist; whereas to adapt a phrase that Arnold applied to Emerson, I should say that Mr. Meredith was not a great novelist; he was a great man who wrote novels.

Immediately after the publication of *Desperate Remedies*, which seemed to teach him, as *Endymion* taught Keats, the highest mysteries of his art, Mr. Hardy entered upon a period of brilliant and splendid production. In three successive years, 1872, 1873, and 1874, he produced three masterpieces — *Under the Greenwood Tree*, *A Pair of Blue Eyes*, and *Far from the Madding Crowd;* followed four years later by what is, perhaps, his greatest contribution to literature, *The Return of the Native*. Even in literary careers that last a long time, there seem to be golden days when the inspiration is unbalked by

obstacles. It is interesting to contemplate the
lengthy row of Scott's novels, and then to remember
that *The Heart of Midlothian*, *The Bride of Lam-
mermoor* and *Ivanhoe* were published in three successive years; to recall that the same brief span
covered in George Eliot's work the production of
Scenes of Clerical Life, *Adam Bede*, and *The Mill
on the Floss;* and one has only to compare what
Mr. Kipling accomplished in 1888, 1889, and 1890
with any other triennial, to discover when he had
what the Methodists call "liberty." Mr. Hardy's
career as a writer has covered about forty years;
omitting his collections of short tales, he has written
fourteen novels; from 1870 to 1880, inclusive, seven
appeared; from 1881 to 1891, five; from 1892 to
1902, two; since 1897 he has published no novels
at all. With that singular and unfortunate perver-
sity which makes authors proudest of their lamest
offspring, Mr. Hardy has apparently abandoned the
novel for poetry and the poetic drama. I suspect
that praise of his verse is sweeter to him than
praise of his fiction; but, although his poems are
interesting for their ideas, and although we all like
the huge *Dynasts* better than we did when we first
saw it, it is a great pity from the economic point of
view that the one man who can write novels better
than anybody else in the same language should deliberately choose to write something else in which

he is at his very best only second rate. The world suffers the same kind of economic loss (less only in degree) that it suffered when Milton spent twenty years of his life in writing prose; and when Tolstoi forsook novels for theology.

It is probable that one reason why Mr. Hardy quit novel-writing was the hostile reception that greeted *Jude the Obscure*. Every great author, except Tennyson, has been able to endure adverse criticism, whether he hits back, like Pope and Byron, or whether he proceeds on his way in silence. But no one has ever enjoyed or ever will enjoy misrepresentation; and there is no doubt that the writer of *Jude* felt that he had been cruelly misunderstood. It is, I think, the worst novel he has ever written, both from the moral and from the artistic point of view; but the novelist was just as sincere in his intention as when he wrote the earlier books. The difficulty is that something of the same change had taken place in his work that is so noticeable in that of Björnson; he had ceased to be a pure artist and had become a propagandist. The fault that marred the splendid novel *Tess of the D'Urbervilles* ruined *Jude the Obscure*. When Mr. Hardy wrote on the title-page of *Tess* the words, "A Pure Woman Faithfully Presented," he issued defiantly the name of a thesis which the story (great, in spite of this) was intended to defend. To a certain extent, his interest in the argument blinded his artistic sense; otherwise he would never have committed the error of hanging his heroine. The mere hanging of a heroine may not be in itself an artistic blunder, for Shakespeare hanged Cordelia. But Mr. Hardy executed Tess because he was bound to see his thesis through. In the prefaces to subsequent editions the author turned on his critics, calling them "sworn discouragers of effort," a phrase that no doubt some of them deserved; and then, like many another man who believes in himself, he punished both critics and the public in the Rehoboam method by issuing *Jude the Obscure*. Instead of being a masterpiece of despair, like *The Return of the Native*, this book is a shriek of rage. Pessimism, which had been a noble ground quality of his earlier writings, is in *Jude* merely hysterical and wholly unconvincing. The author takes obvious pains to make things come out wrong; as in melodramas and childish romances, the law of causation is suspended in the interest of the hero's welfare. Animalism, which had partially disfigured *Tess*, became gross and revolting in *Jude*; and the representation of marriage and the relations between men and women, instead of being a picture of life, resembled a caricature. It is a matter of sincere regret that Mr. Hardy has stopped novel-writing, but we want no more *Judes*. Didactic pessimism is not good for the novel.

The Well-Beloved, published in 1897, but really a revision of an earlier tale, is in a way a triumph of Art. The plot is simply absurd, almost as whimsical as anything in *Alice in Wonderland.* A man proposes to a young girl and is rejected; when her daughter is grown, he proposes to the representative of the second generation, and with the same ill fortune. When *her* daughter reaches maturity, he tries the third woman in line and without success. His perseverance was equalled only by his bad luck, as so often happens in Mr. Hardy's stories. And yet, with a plot that would wreck any other novelist, the author constructed a powerful and beautifully written novel. It is as though the architect had taken a wretched plan and yet somehow contrived to erect on its false lines a handsome building. The book has naturally added nothing to his reputation, but as a *tour de force* it is hard to surpass.

It is pleasant to remember that a man's opinion of his own work has nothing to do with its final success and that his best creations cannot be injured by his worst. Tolstoi may be ashamed of having written *Anna Karenina,* and may insist that his sociological tracts are superior productions, but we know better; and rejoice in his powerlessness to efface his own masterpieces. We may honestly think that we should be ashamed to put our own names to such stuff as *Little Dorrit,* but that does **not** prevent us from admiring the splendid genius that produced *David Copperfield* and *Great Expectations*. Mr. Hardy may believe that *Jude the Obscure* represents his zenith as a novelist, and that his poems are still greater literature; but one reading of *Jude* suffices, while we never tire of rereading *Far from the Madding Crowd* and *The Return of the Native*. Probably no publisher's announcement in the world to-day would cause more pleasure to English-speaking people than the announcement that Thomas Hardy was at work on a Wessex novel with characters of the familiar kind.

For *The Dynasts*, which covers the map of Europe, transcends the sky, and deals with world-conquerors, is not nearly so great a world-drama as *A Pair of Blue Eyes*, that is circumscribed in a small corner of a small island, and treats exclusively of a little group of commonplace persons. Literature deals with a constant — human nature, which is the same in Wessex as in Vienna. As the late Mr. Clyde Fitch used to say, it is not the great writers that have great things happen to them; the great things happen to the ordinary people they portray. Mr. Hardy selected a few of the southwestern counties of England as the stage for his prose dramas; to this locality he for the first time, in *Far from the Madding Crowd*, gave the name Wessex, a name now wholly fictitious, but which his creative im-

agination has made so real that it is constantly
and seriously spoken of as though it were English
geography. In these smiling valleys and quiet
rural scenes, "while the earth keeps up her terrible
composure," the farmers and milkmaids hold us
spellbound as they struggle in awful passion. The
author of the drama stands aloof, making no effort
to guide his characters from temptation, folly, and
disaster, and offering no explanation to the spectators,
who are thrilled with pity and fear. But one feels
that he loves and hates his children as we do, and
that he correctly gauges their moral value. The
very narrowness of the scene increases the intensity
of the play. The rustic cackle of his bourg drowns
the murmur of the world.

Mr. Hardy's knowledge of and sympathy with
nature is of course obvious to all readers, but it is
none the less impressive as we once more open
books that we have read many times. There are
incidentally few novelists who repay one so richly
for repeated perusals. He seems as inexhaustible
as nature herself, and he grows stale no faster than
the repetition of the seasons. It is perhaps rather
curious that a man who finds nature so absolutely
inexorable and indifferent to human suffering should
love her so well. But every man must love something greater than himself, and as Mr. Hardy had
no God, he has drawn close to the world of trees,

plains, and rivers. His intimacy with nature is almost uncanny. Nature is not merely a background in his stories, it is often an active agent. There are striking characters in *The Return of the Native*, but the greatest character in the book is Egdon Heath. The opening chapter, which gives the famous picture of the Heath, is like an overture to a great music-drama. The *Heath-motif* is repeated again and again in the story. It has a personality of its own, and affects the fortunes and the hearts of all human beings who dwell in its proximity. If one stands to-day on the edge of this Heath at the twilight hour, just at the moment when Darkness is conquering Light — the moment chosen by Mr. Hardy for the first chapter — one realises its significance and its possibilities. In *Tess of the D'Urbervilles* the intercourse between man and nature is set forth with amazing power. The different seasons act as chorus to the human tragedy. In *The Woodlanders* the trees seem like separate individualities. To me a tree has become a different thing since I first read this particular novel.

Even before he took up the study of architecture, Mr. Hardy's unconscious training as a novelist began. When he was a small boy, the Dorchester girls found him useful in a way that recalls the services of that reliable child, Samuel Richardson. These village maids, in their various love-affairs,

which necessitated a large amount of private corre-
spondence, employed young Hardy as amanuensis.
He did not, like his great predecessor, compose their
epistles; but he held the pen, and faithfully recorded the inspiration of Love, as it flowed warm
from the lips of passionate youth. In this manner,
the almost sexless boy was enabled to look clear-eyed
into the very heart of palpitating young womanhood,
and to express accurately its most gentle and most
stormy emotions; just as the white voice of a choir-
child repeats with precision the thrilling notes of
religious passion. These early experiences were undoubtedly of the highest value in later years; indeed,
as the boy grew a little older, it is probable that the
impression deepened. Mr. Hardy is fond of depicting the vague, half-conscious longing of a boy
to be near a beautiful woman; everyone will remember the contract between Eustacia and her
youthful admirer, by which he was to hold her hand
for a stipulated number of minutes. Mr. Hardy's
women are full of tenderness and full of caprice;
and whatever feminine readers may think of them,
they are usually irresistible to the masculine mind.
It has been said, indeed, that he is primarily a man's
novelist, as Mrs. Ward is perhaps a woman's; he
does not represent his women as marvels of intellectual splendour, or in queenly domination over the
society in which they move. They are more apt to

be the victims of their own affectionate hearts. One female reader, exasperated at this succession of portraits, wrote on the margin of one of Mr. Hardy's novels that she took from a circulating library, "Oh, how I *hate* Thomas Hardy!" This is an interesting gloss, even if we do not add meanly that it bears witness to the truth of the picture. Elfride, Bathsheba, Eustacia, Lady Constantine, Marty South, and Tess are of varied social rank and wealth; but they are all alike in humble prostration before the man they love. Mr. Hardy takes particular pleasure in representing them as swayed by sudden and constantly changing caprices; one has only to recall the charming Bathsheba Everdene, and her various attitudes toward the three men who admire her — Troy, Boldwood, and Gabriel Oak. Mr. Hardy's heroines change their minds oftener than they change their clothes; but in whatever material or mental presentment, they never lack attraction. And they all resemble their maker in one respect; at heart every one of them is a Pagan. They vary greatly in constancy and in general strength of character; but it is human passion, and not religion, that is the mainspring of their lives. He has never drawn a truly spiritual woman, like Browning's Pompilia.

His best men, from the moral point of view, are closest to the soil. Gabriel Oak, in *Far from the Madding Crowd*, and Venn, in *The Return of the*

Native, are, on the whole, his noblest characters. Oak is a shepherd and Venn is a reddleman; their sincerity, charity, and fine sense of honour have never been injured by what is called polite society. And Mr. Hardy, the stingiest author toward his characters, has not entirely withheld reward from these two. Henry Knight and Angel Clare, who have whatever advantages civilisation is supposed to give, are certainly not villains; they are men of the loftiest ideals; but if each had been a deliberate black-hearted villain, he could not have treated the innocent woman who loved him with more ugly cruelty. Compared with Oak and Venn, this precious pair of prigs are seen to have only the righteousness of the Scribes and Pharisees; a righteousness that is of little help in the cruel emergencies of life. Along with them must stand Clym Yeobright, another slave to moral theory, who quite naturally ends his days as an itinerant preacher. The real villains in Mr. Hardy's novels, Sergeant Troy, young Dare, and Alec D'Urberville, seem the least natural and the most machine-made of all his characters.

Mr. Hardy's pessimism is a picturesque and splendid contribution to modern fiction. We should be as grateful for it in this field as we are to Schopenhauer in the domain of metaphysics. I am no pessimist myself, but I had rather read Schopenhauer than all the rest of the philosophers put together, Plato alone excepted. The pessimism of Mr. Hardy resembles that of Schopenhauer in being absolutely thorough and absolutely candid; it makes the world as darkly superb and as terribly interesting as a Greek drama. It is wholly worth while to get this point of view; and if in practical life one does not really believe in it, it is capable of yielding much pleasure. After finishing one of Mr. Hardy's novels, one has all the delight of waking from an impressive but horrible dream, and feeling through the dissolving vision the real friendliness of the good old earth. It is like coming home from an adequate performance of *King Lear*, which we would not have missed for anything. There are so many make-believe pessimists, so many whose pessimism is a sham and a pose, which will not stand for a moment in a real crisis, that we cannot withhold admiration for such pessimism as Mr. Hardy's, which is fundamental and sincere. To him the Christian religion and what we call the grace of God have not the slightest shade of meaning; he is as absolute a Pagan as though he had written four thousand years before Christ. This is something almost refreshing, because it is so entirely different from the hypocrisy and cant, the pretence of pessimism, so familiar to us in the works of modern writers; and so inconsistent with their daily life.

Mr. Hardy's pessimism is the one deep-seated conviction of his whole intellectual process.

I once saw a print of a cartoon drawn by a contemporary Dresden artist, Herr Sascha Schneider. It was called "The Helplessness of Man against Destiny." We see a quite naked man, standing with his back to us; his head is bowed in hopeless resignation; heavy manacles are about his wrists, to which chains are attached, that lead to some fastening in the ground. Directly before him, with hideous hands, that now almost entirely surround the little circle where he stands in dejection, crawls flatly toward him a prodigious, shapeless monster, with his horrid narrow eyes fixed on his defenceless human prey. And the man is so conscious of his tether, that even in the very presence of the unspeakably awful object, *the chains hang loose!* He may have tried them once, but he has since given up. The monster is Destiny; and the real meaning of the picture is seen in the eyes, nose, and mouth of the loathsome beast. There is not only no sympathy and no intelligence there; there is an expression far more terrible than the evident lust to devour; there is plainly the *sense of humour* shown on this hideous face. The contrast between the limitless strength of the monster and the utter weakness of the man, flavours the stupidity of Destiny with the zest of humour.

Now this is a correct picture of life as Mr. Hardy sees it. His God is a kind of insane child, who cackles foolishly as he destroys the most precious objects. Some years ago I met a man entirely blind. He said that early in life he had lost the sight of one eye by an accident; and that years later, as he held a little child on his lap, the infant, in rare good humour, playfully poked the point of a pair of scissors into the other, thus destroying his sight for ever. So long an interval had elapsed since this second and final catastrophe, that the man spoke of it without the slightest excitement or resentment. The child with the scissors might well represent Hardy's conception of God. Destiny is whimsical, rather than definitely malicious; for Destiny has not sufficient intelligence even to be systematically bad. We smile at Caliban's natural theology, as he composes his treatise on Setebos; but his God is the same who disposes of man's proposals in the stories of our novelist.

> "In which feat, if his leg snapped, brittle clay,
>   And he lay stupid-like, — why, I should laugh;
> And if he, spying me, should fall to weep,
> Beseech me to be good, repair his wrong,
> Bid his poor leg smart less or grow again, —
> Well, as the chance were, this might take or else
> Not take my fancy. . . .
>   'Thinketh, such shows nor right nor wrong in Him,
> Nor kind, nor cruel: He is strong and Lord."

Mr. Hardy believes that, morally, men and women are immensely superior to God; for all the good qualities that we attribute to Him in prayer are human, not divine. He in his loneliness is totally devoid of the sense of right and wrong, and knows neither justice nor mercy. His poem *New Year's Eve* [1] clearly expresses his theology.

Mr. Hardy's pessimism is not in the least personal, nor has it risen from any sorrow or disappointment in his own life. It is both philosophic and temperamental. He cannot see nature in any other way. To venture a guess, I think his pessimism is mainly caused by his deep, manly tenderness for all forms of human and animal life and by an almost abnormal sympathy. His intense love for bird and beast is well known; many a stray cat and hurt dog have found in him a protector and a refuge. He firmly believes that the sport of shooting is wicked, and he has repeatedly joined in practical measures to waken the public conscience on this subject. As a spectator of human history, he sees life as a vast tragedy, with men and women emerging from nothingness, suffering acute physical and mental sorrow, and then passing into nothingness again. To his sympathetic mind, the creed of optimism is a ribald insult to the pain of humanity and devout piety merely absurd. To hear these suffering men

[1] See Appendix.

and women utter prayers of devotion and sing hymns of adoration to the Power whence comes all their anguish is to him a veritable abdication of reason and common sense. God simply does not deserve it, and he for one will have the courage to say so. He will not stand by and see humanity submit so tamely to so heartless a tyrant. For, although Mr. Hardy is a pessimist, he has not the least tincture of cynicism. If one analyses his novels carefully, one will see that he seldom shows scorn for his characters; his contempt is almost exclusively devoted to God. Sometimes the evil fate that his characters suffer is caused by the very composition of their mind, as is seen in *A Pair of Blue Eyes;* again it is no positive human agency, but rather an Æschylean conception of hidden forces, as in *The Return of the Native;* but in neither case is humanity to blame.

This pessimism has one curious effect that adds greatly to the reader's interest when he takes up an hitherto unread novel by our author. The majority of works of fiction end happily; indeed, many are so badly written that any ending cannot be considered unfortunate. But with most novelists we have a sense of security. We know that, no matter what difficulties the hero and heroine may encounter, the unseen hand of their maker will guide them eventually to paths of pleasantness and peace. Mr.

Hardy inspires no such confidence. In reading Trollope, one smiles at a cloud of danger, knowing it will soon pass over; but after reading *A Pair of Blue Eyes*, or *Tess*, one follows the fortunes of young Somerset in *A Laodicean* with constant fluctuation of faint hope and real terror; for we know that with Mr. Hardy the worst may happen at any moment.

However dark may be his conception of life, Mr. Hardy's sense of humour is unexcelled by his contemporaries in its subtlety of feeling and charm of expression. His rustics, who have long received and deserved the epithet "Shakespearian," arouse in every reader harmless and wholesome delight. The shadow of the tragedy lifts in these wonderful pages, for Mr. Hardy's laughter reminds one of what Carlyle said of Shakespeare's: it is like sunshine on the deep sea. The childlike sincerity of these shepherd farmers, the candour of their repartee and their appraisal of gentle-folk are as irresistible as their patience and equable temper. Everyone in the community seems to find his proper mental and moral level. And their infrequent fits of irritation are as pleasant as their more solemn moods. We can all sympathise (I hope) with the despair of Joseph Poorgrass: "I was sitting at home looking for Ephesians and says I to myself, 'Tis nothing but Corinthians and Thessalonians in this danged Testament!"

III

WILLIAM DEAN HOWELLS

Born in a little village in Ohio over seventy years ago, and growing up with small Latin and less Greek, Mr. Howells may fairly be called a self-educated man. Just why the epithet "self-made" should be applied to those non-college-graduates who succeed in business, and withheld from those who succeed in poetry and fiction, seems not entirely clear. Perhaps it is tacitly assumed that those who become captains of industry achieve prominence without divine assistance; whereas men of letters, with or without early advantages, and whether grateful or not, have unconscious communication with hidden forces. Be this as it may, the boy Howells had little schooling and no college. All the public institutions in the world, however, are but a poor makeshift in the absence of good home training; and the future novelist's father was the right sort of man and had the right sort of occupation to stimulate a clever and ambitious son. The elder Howells was the editor of a country newspaper, which, like a country doctor, makes up in variety of information what it loses in spread of influence. The boy was a compositor before he was a composer, as plenty of literary men since Richardson have been; he helped to set up lyrics, news items, local gossip, the funny column, and patent medicine advertisements. From mechanical he passed to original work, both in his father's office and in other sanctums about the state; sometimes acting not only as contributor, but "moulding public opinion" from the editor's chair. And indeed he has never entirely stepped out of the editorial rôle. During an amazingly busy life as novelist, dramatist, poet, and foreign diplomat, Mr. Howells has acted as editorial writer on the *Nation*, the *Atlantic*, the *Cosmopolitan Magazine*, and *Harper's Monthly*. I think he would sometimes be appalled at the prodigious amount of merely "timely" articles that he has written, were it not for the fact that during his long career he has never published a single line of which he need feel ashamed.

Type-setters and printers are commonly men of ideas, who have interesting minds, and are good to talk with. Mr. Howells was certainly no exception to the rule, and to the foundation of his early education as a compositor and journalist he added four years of study of the Italian language and literature in the pleasant environment of Venice. He has always been a man of peace; and it is interesting to remember that during the four years of tumultuous and bloody civil war, Mr. Howells was serving his country as a United States Consul in Italy, and at the same time preparing to add to the kind of fame she most sorely needs. The "woman-country" never meant to him what it signified to Browning; but it has always been an inspiration, and he would have been a different person without this foreign influence. Besides some critical and scholarly works on Italian literature, much of his subsequent writing has been done beyond the Alps, and the plot of one of his foremost novels develops on the streets of Florence. And in another and wholly delightful story, we have the keen pleasure of seeing Italian life and society through the eyes of Lydia Blood.

He formally began a literary career by the composition of a volume of poems, as Blackmore, Hardy, Meredith, and many other novelists have seen fit to do. He is not widely known as a poet to-day, though all his life he has written more or less verse without achieving distinction; for he is essentially a *prosateur*. In 1872, twelve years after the appearance of his book of poems, came his first successful novel, *Their Wedding Journey*. This story is written in the style that is responsible for its author's fame and popularity; it is thoroughly typical of the whole first part of his novel-production. It has that quiet stingless humour, clever dialogue, and wholesome charm, that all readers of Mr. Howells associate with his name. In other words, it is a clear manifestation of his own personality. Now as to the permanent value and final place in literature of these American novels, critics may differ; but there can be only one opinion of the man who wrote them.

The personality of Mr. Howells, as shown both in his objective novels and in his subjective literary confessions, is one that irresistibly commands our highest respect and our warmest affection. A simple, democratic, unaffected, modest, kindly, humorous, healthy soul, with a rare combination of rugged virility and extreme refinement. It is exceedingly fortunate for America that such a man has for so many years by common consent, at home and abroad, been regarded as the Dean of American Letters. He has had more influence on the output of fiction in America than any other living man. This influence has been entirely wholesome, from the standpoint of both morals and Art. He has consistently stood for Reticent Realism. He has ridiculed what he is fond of calling "romantic rot," and his own novels have been a silent but emphatic protest against "mentioning the unmentionable." Every now and then there has risen a violent revolt against his leadership, the latest outspoken attack coming from a novelist of distinction, Gertrude Atherton. In the year 1907 she relieved her mind by declaring that Mr. Howells has been and is a writer for boarding-school misses; that he has never penetrated deeply into life; and that not only has his own timidity prevented him from courageously revealing the hearts of men and women, but that his position of power and influence has cast a blight on American fiction. Thanks to him, she insists, American novels are pale and colourless productions, and are known the world over for their tameness and insipidity. Mrs. Atherton has been supported in this revolt by many very young literary aspirants, who lack her wisdom and her experience, and whose chief dislike of Mr. Howells, when finally analysed, seems to be directed against his intense ethical earnestness. For, at heart, Mr. Howells resembles most Anglo-Saxon novelists in being a moralist.

It is true that American novelists and playwrights are at one great disadvantage as compared with contemporary Continental writers. Owing to the public conscience, they are compelled to work in a limited field. The things that we leave to medical specialists and to alienists are staple subject-matter in high-class French and German fiction. In a

European dictionary there is no such word as "reserve." French writers like Brieux protest that American conceptions of French morals are based on the reading of French books whose authors have no standing in Paris, and whose very names are unknown to their countrymen. But this protest fades before facts. The facts are that Parisian novelists and dramatists of the highest literary and social distinction, who are awarded national prizes, admitted to the French Academy, and who receive all sorts of public honours, write and publish books, which, if produced in the United States by an American, would bar him from the houses and from the society of many decent people, and might cause his arrest. At any rate, he would be regarded as a criminal rather than as a hero. I have in mind plays by Donnay, recently elected to the French Academy; plays by Capus, who stands high in public regard; novels by Regnier, who has received all sorts of honours. These men are certainly not fourth- and fifth-class writers; they are thoroughly representative of Parisian literary taste. Regnier has not hesitated to write, and the editors have not hesitated to accept, for the periodical *L'Illustration*, which goes into family circles everywhere, a novel that could not possibly be published in any respectable magazine in America. I do not say that Americans are one peg higher in morality than Frenchmen; it may be that we are hypocrites, and that the French are models of virtue; but the difference in moral tone between the average American play or novel and that produced in Paris is simply enormous.

The modern German novel is no better than the French. Last night I finished reading Sudermann's long and powerful story, *Das hohe Lied*. I could not help thinking how entirely different it is in its subject-matter, in its characters, in its scenes, and in its atmosphere, from the average American novel. Now of course the subject that arouses the most instant interest from all classes of people, both young and old, innocent and guilty, is the subject of sex. A large number of modern successful French and German novels and plays contain no other matter of any real importance — and would be intolerably dull were it not for their dealing with sexual crimes. The Continental writer is barred by no restraint; when he has nothing to say, as is very often the case, he simply plays his trump card. The American, however, is not permitted to penetrate beyond the bounds of decency; which shuts him off from the chief field where European writers dwell. He must somehow make his novel interesting to his readers, just as a man is expected to make himself interesting in social conversation, without recourse to pruriency or obscenity.

WILLIAM DEAN HOWELLS

Leaving out of debate for a moment the moral aspect of Art, is it necessarily true that novels which plunge freely into sex questions are a more faithful representation of life than those that observe the limits of good taste? I think not. The men and women in many Continental stories have apparently nothing to do except to gratify their passions. All the thousand and one details that make up the daily routine of the average person are sacrificed to emphasise one thing; but this, even in most degraded Sybarites, would be only a part of their actual activity. I believe that *A Modern Instance* is just as true to life as *Bel-Ami*. It would really be a misfortune if Mrs. Atherton could have her way; for then American novelists would copy the faults of European writers instead of their virtues. The reason why French plays and French novels are generally superior to American is not because they are indecent; and we shall never raise our standard merely by copying foreign immorality. The superiority of the French is an intellectual and artistic superiority; they excel us in literary style. If we are to imitate them, let us imitate their virtues and not their defects, even though the task in this case be infinitely more difficult.

And, granting what Mrs. Atherton says, that the reticence of American fiction is owing largely to the influence of Mr. Howells, have we not every reason to be grateful to him? Has not the modern novel a tremendous influence in education, and do we really wish to see young men and women, boys and girls, reading stories that deal mainly with sex? Is it well that they should abandon Dickens, Thackeray, and Stevenson, for the novel in vogue on the Continent? It is often said that French fiction is intended only for seasoned readers, and is carefully kept from youth. But this is gammon, and should deceive only the grossly ignorant. As if anything nowadays could be kept from youth! With the exception of girls who are very strictly brought up, young people in Europe have the utmost freedom in reading. In one of Regnier's novels, which purports to be autobiographical, the favourite bedside book of the boy in his teens is *Mademoiselle de Maupin*. In a secret ballot vote recently taken by a Russian periodical, to discover who are the most popular novelists with high-school boys and girls in Russia, it appeared that of all foreign writers Guy de Maupassant stood first. Is this really a desirable state of affairs? Suppose it be true, as it probably is, that the average Russian, German, or French boy of seventeen is intellectually more mature than his English or American contemporary — are we willing to make the physical and moral sacrifice for the merely mental advance? Is it not better that our boys should be playing football

and reading *Treasure Island*, than that they should
be spending their leisure hours in the manner described by Regnier?

Mr. Howells's creed in Art is perhaps more open
to criticism than his creed in Ethics. His artistic
creed is narrow, strict, and definite. He has ex-
pressed it in his essays, and exemplified it in his
novels. His two doctrinal works, *Criticism and
Fiction*, and *My Literary Passions*, resemble Zola's
Le Roman Expérimental in dogmatic limitation.
The creed of Mr. Howells is realism, which he has
not only faithfully followed in his creative work,
but which he uses as a standard by which to measure
the value of other novelists, both living and dead.
As genius always refuses to be measured by any
standard, and usually defies classification, Mr.
Howells's literary estimates of other men's work
are far more valuable as self-revelation than as
adequate appraisal. Indeed, some of his criticisms
seem bizarre. Where works of fiction do not run
counter to his literary dogmas, he is abundantly
sympathetic and more than generous; many a
struggling young writer has cause to bless him for
powerful assistance; apparently there has never
been one grain of envy, jealousy, or meanness in the
mind of our American dean. But, broadly speaking,
Mr. Howells has not the true critical mind, which
places itself for the moment in the mental attitude

of the author criticised; he is primarily a creative rather than a critical writer. Here he is in curious opposition to his friend and contemporary, Henry James. Mr. James is a natural-born critic, one of the best America has ever produced. His essay on Balzac was a masterpiece. His intellectual power is far more critical than creative; as a novelist, he seems quite inferior to Mr. Howells. And his best story, the little sketch, *Daisy Miller*, was properly called by its author a "study."

Mr. Howells's literary career has two rather definite periods. The break was caused largely by the influence of Tolstoi. The earlier novels are more purely artistic; they are accurate representations of American characters, for the most part joyous in mood, full of genuine humour, and natural charm. A story absolutely expressive of the author as we used to know him is *The Lady of the Aroostook*. As a sympathetic and delightful portrayal of a New England country girl, this book is one of his best productions. The voyage across the Atlantic; the surprise caused by Lydia's name and appearance, and homely conversation. "I want to know!" cried Lydia. The second surprise caused by her splendid singing voice. The third surprise caused to the sophisticated young gentleman by discovering that he was in love with her. His rapture at his glorious good-fortune in saving the drunken wretch from drowning, thus acting as hero before his lady's eyes; her virginal experiences in Italy; the final happy consummation — all this is in Mr. Howells's best vein, the Howells of thirty years ago. The story is full of observation, cerebration, and human affection. As Professor Beers has remarked, if Mr. Howells knows his countrymen no more intimately than does Henry James, at least he loves them better. This charming novel was rapidly followed in the next few years by a succession of books that are at once good to read, and of permanent value as reflections of American life, manners, and morals. These were *A Modern Instance*, *A Woman's Reason*, *The Rise of Silas Lapham*, and *Indian Summer;* making a literary harvest of which not only their author, but all Americans, have reason to be justly proud.

Somewhere along in the eighties Mr. Howells came fully within the grasp of the mighty influence of Tolstoi, an influence, which, no matter how beneficial in certain ways, has not been an unmixed blessing on his foreign disciples. What the American owes to the great Russian, and how warm is his gratitude therefor, any one may see for himself by reading *My Literary Passions*. It is indeed difficult to praise the maker of *Anna Karenina* too highly; but nobody wanted Mr. Howells to become a lesser Tolstoi. When we wish to read Tolstoi, we know where to find him; we wish Mr. Howells to remain his own self, shrewdly observant, and kindly humorous. The latter novels of the American show the same kind of change that took place in Björnson, that has also characterised Bourget; it is the partial abandonment of the novel as an art form, and its employment as a social, political, or religious tract. Mr. Howells's saving sense of humour has kept him from dull extremes; but when *A Hazard of New Fortunes* appeared, we knew that there was more in the title than the writer intended; our old friend had put on Saul's armour. As has been suggested above, this change was not entirely an individual one; it was symptomatic of the development of the modern novel all over the world. But in this instance it seemed particularly regrettable. We have our fill of strikes and labour troubles in the daily newspaper, without going to our novelist for them. With one exception, it is probable that not a single one of Mr. Howells's novels published during the last twenty years is as good, from the artistic and literary point of view, as the admirable work he produced before 1889. The exception is *The Kentons* (1902), in which he returned to his earlier manner, in a triumphant way that showed he had not lost his skill. Indeed, there is no trace of decay in the other books of his late years; there is merely a loss of charm.

WILLIAM DEAN HOWELLS

I think that *Indian Summer*, despite its immense popularity at the time of publication, has never received the high praise it really deserves. It is written in a positive glow of artistic creation. I believe that of all its author's works, it is the one whose composition he most keenly enjoyed. The conversations — always a great feature of his stories — are immensely clever; I suspect that as he wrote them he was often agreeably surprised at his own inspiration. The three characters, the middle-aged man and woman, and the romantic young girl, are admirably set off; no one has ever better shown the fact that it is quite possible for one to imagine oneself in love when really one is fancy-free. The delicate shades of jealousy in the intimate talks between the two women are exquisitely done; the experience of the grown woman contrasting finely with the imagination of the young girl. The difference between a man of forty and a woman of twenty, shown here not in heavy tragedy, but in the innumerable, convincing details of daily human intercourse, is finely emphasised; and we can feel the great relief of both when the engagement tie is broken. This story in its way is a masterpiece; and anyone who lacks enthusiasm for its author ought to read it again.

His most powerful novel is probably *A Modern Instance*. This, like many American and English fictions, first appeared in serial form — a fact that should be known before one indulges in criticism. The old objection to this method was that it led the writer to attempt to end each section dramatically, leaving the reader with a sharp appetite for more. The movement of the narrative, when the book was finally published as a whole, resembled a series of jumps. Someone has said, that even so fine a novel as *Far from the Madding Crowd* was a succession of brilliant leaps; whether or not this was caused by its original serial printing, I do not know. This difficulty would never appear in Mr. Howells, at all events; because his stories do not impress us by their special dramatic scenes, or supreme moments, but rather by their completeness. The other objection, however, has some force here — the fact that details may be extended beyond their artistic proportion, in a manner that does not militate against the separate instalments, but is seen to mar the book as a whole. The logging camp incident in *A Modern Instance* is prolonged to a fault. Proportion is sacrificed to realism. From this point of view, it is well to remember that *The Newcomes* appeared in single numbers, whereas *Henry Esmond* was published originally as a complete work.

But this slight defect is more than atoned for by the power shown in the depiction of character. This is a study of degeneration, not dealing with remote characters in far-off historical situations, but brought home to our very doors. One feels that this dreadful fate might happen to one's neighbours — might happen to oneself. It seems to me a greater book in every way than *Romola*, though I am not prepared to say that Mr. Howells is a greater novelist than George Eliot. There is all the difference between Tito Melema and Bartley Hubbard that there is between a fancy picture and a portrait. Mr. Howells is fond of using Shakespearian quotations as titles; witness *The Counterfeit Presentment, The Undiscovered Country, The Quality of Mercy,* and *A Modern Instance.* Now the word "modern," as every student of Shakespeare knows, means in the poet's works almost the opposite of what it signifies to-day. "Full of wise saws and modern instances" is equivalent to saying prosaically, "full of sententious proverbs and old, trite illustrations." In the Shakespearian sense, Mr. Howells's title might be translated "A Familiar Example" — for it is not only a story of modern American life, it portrays what is unfortunately an instance all too familiar. Bartley Hubbard is the typical representative of the "smart" young American. He is not in the least odious when we first make his acquaintance. His skill in address and in adaptation to society assure his instant popularity; and at heart he is a good fellow, quite unlike a designing villain. He would rather do right than do wrong, provided both are equally convenient. He simply follows the line of least resistance. Nor is he by nature a Bohemian; he loves Marcia, is proud of her fresh beauty, and enjoys domestic life. Then he has the fascinating quality of true humour. His conversations with his wife, when he is free from worry, are exceedingly attractive to the impersonal listener. He is just like thousands of clever young American journalists — quick-witted, enterprising, energetic, with a sure nose for news; there is, in fact, only one thing the matter with Bartley. Although, when life is flowing evenly, he does not realise his deficiency, he actually has at heart no moral principle, no ethical sense, no honour. The career of such a man will depend entirely upon circumstances; because his standard of virtue is not where it should be, within his own mind, but without. Like many other men, he can resist anything but temptation. Whether he will become a good citizen or a blackleg, depends not in the least upon himself, but wholly upon the events through which he moves. Had he married exactly the right sort of girl, and had some rich uncle left the young couple a fortune, it is probable that neither his friends, nor his wife, nor even he himself, would have guessed at his capacity for evil. He would have remained popular in the community, and died both lamented and respected. But the difficulty is that he did not marry wisely, and he subsequently became short of cash. Now, as some writer has said, it does not matter so much whether a man marries with wisdom or the reverse, nor whether he behaves in other emergencies with prudence or folly; what really matters is how he behaves himself *after* the marriage, or after any other crisis where he may have chosen foolishly. But Bartley, like many other easy-going youths, was no man for adverse circumstances. Almost imperceptibly at first his degeneration begins; his handsome figure shows a touch of grossness; the refinement in his face becomes blurred; drinking ceases to be a pleasure, and becomes a habit. Meanwhile, as what he calls his bad luck increases, quarrels with his wife become more frequent; try as he will, there is always a sheaf of unpaid bills at the end of the month; his home loses its charm. The mental and spiritual decline of the man is shown repulsively by his physical appearance. No one who has read the book can possibly forget his broad back as he sits in the courtroom, and the horrible ring of fat that hangs over his collar. The devil has done his work with such technique that Bartley as we first see him, and Bartley as we last see him, seem to be two utterly different and distinct persons and personalities; it is with an irrepressible shudder that we recall the time when this coarse, fat sot was a slender, graceful young man, who charmed all acquaintances by his ease of manner and winsome conversation. And yet, as one looks back over his life, every stage in the transition is clear, logical, and wholly natural.

From another point of view this novel is a study of the passion of jealousy. No other American novel, so far as I know, has given so accurate a picture of the gradual and subtle poisoning produced by this emotion, and only one American play, — Clyde Fitch's thoughtful and powerful drama, *The Girl with the Green Eyes*. It is curious that jealousy, so sinister and terrible in its effects on character, should usually appear on the stage and in fiction as comic. It is seldom employed as a leading motive in tragedy, though Shakespeare showed its possibilities; but one frequently sees it in broad farce. Of all the passions, there is none which has less mirth than jealousy. It is fundamentally tragic; and in *A Modern Instance*, we see the evil transformation it works in Marcia, and its force in accelerating her husband's degeneration. Marcia is an example of the wish of Keats — she lives a life of sensations rather than of thoughts; and jealousy can be conquered only by mental power, never by emotional. Marcia has no intellectual resources; her love for her husband is her whole existence. She has no

more mind than many another American country
girl who comes home from boarding-school. As
one critic has pointed out, "she has not yet emerged
from the elemental condition of womanhood."
Jealousy is, of course, an "animal quality," and
Marcia, without knowing it, is simply a tamed,
pretty, affectionate young animal. Her jealousy
is entirely without foundation, but it causes her the
most excruciating torment, and constantly widens
the breach between herself and the man she loves.
If she had only married Halleck! She would never
have been jealous with him. But jealousy is like
an ugly weed in a beautiful garden; it exists only
where there is love. And a girl like Marcia could
never have returned the love of a stodgy man like
Halleck. One cannot help asking three vain
questions as one contemplates the ruins of her
happiness and sees the cause. If she had never
met Bartley, and had married Halleck, would she
have been better off? are we to understand that
she is finally saved by Halleck? and if so, what is
the nature of her salvation?

The old sceptical lawyer, Marcia's father, is one
of the most convincing characters that Mr. Howells
has ever drawn. Those who have lived in New
England know this man, for they have seen him
often. He is shrewd, silent, practical, undemon-
strative, yet his unspoken love for his daughter is

almost terrible in its intensity, and finally brings him to the grave. Although he admires young Bartley's cleverness, he would have admired him more had he been less clever. He has a sure instinct against the young man from the start, and knows there can be only one outcome of such a marriage; because he is better acquainted with the real character of husband and wife than they are with themselves. Squire Gaylord is a person of whose creation any novelist in the history of fiction might be proud.

When *A Modern Instance* was first published, a contemporary review called it "a book that all praise but none like." I imagine that the unpleasant sensations it awakens in every reader are like those roused by Mr. Barrie's *Sentimental Tommy*. The picture is simply too faithful to be agreeable. Everyone beholds his own faults and tendencies clearly portrayed, and the result is quite other than reassuring. The book finds us all at home. But, as Gogol, the great Russian, used to say, quoting an old Slavonic proverb, "We must not blame the mirror if the face looks ugly."

It is both instructive and entertaining to try the effect of this novel on a representative group of American college undergraduates. Those who had lived in New England villages, and were familiar with the scenes described, were loud in their praises

of the background, and of the Gaylord family.
One young man remarked — he was at Yale — "I
know a young journalist who was last year at Harvard, who is going to the devil in very much the
same way." Another said, with an experience
hardly consonant with his years, that he had known
women just as jealous as Marcia. Most of them,
however, believed that her jealousy was grossly
exaggerated; it looks so like folly to those yet un-
touched by the passion of love. Another truthful
and modest youth said pathetically, "I am too
young to appreciate this book." Still another
remarked with rare lucidity and definiteness of
penetration, "In reading this story somehow something struck me unfavourably." Minor improba-
bilities in the novel produced the greatest shock —
the hot-scotch episode seemed quite impossible,
and Mr. Howells was thought to be a poor judge
of the effects of whiskey. But the criticism I enjoyed most came from the undergraduate who said
in all sincerity, "I think this is a very good book
for young ladies to read before getting married."
So indeed it is.

In the year 1902, by the publication of *The
Kentons*, Mr. Howells gave us a most delightful
surprise. It was like the return of an old friend
from a far journey. In literature it was as though
Björnson should publish a story like *A Happy Boy*,

or as though Mr. Hardy should give us a tale like *Under the Greenwood Tree*. *The Kentons* is a thoroughly charming international novel, containing the pleasant adventures of an Ohio family on the ocean liner and in Europe, written in the *Aroostook* style, sparkling with humour, and rich in sympathy and tenderness. Political, social, and ethical problems are conspicuously absent, and the only material used by the writer is human nature. This is one of the best books he has ever written; it has all the charm of *Their Wedding Journey*, plus the wisdom and observation that come only by years. It is wholesome, healthy, realistic; a thoroughly representative American novel from a master's hand. In a French *roman*, Bittredge would of course have been a libertine, and one of the girls ruined by him. In *The Kentons*, he is merely *fresh*, and though he causes some trouble, everybody in the end is better off for the experience. Mr. Howells seems especially to dislike *Frechheit* in young men, and he has made the vulgarity and assurance of Bittredge both offensive and absurd. We have too many Bittredges in the United States; and some of them do not lose their bittredgidity with advancing years.

The five members of the Kenton family are wonderfully well drawn, and are just such people as we fortunately meet every day. The purity

and sweetness of married and family life are beautifully exemplified here; they are exactly what we see in thousands of American homes, and constitute the real answer to modern attacks on the conjugal relation. The judge and his wife are two companions, growing old together in simplicity and innocence, happy in the truest sense — loving each other far more in age than in youth, which is perfectly natural in life if not in fiction; because every day they become more necessary to each other and have common interests extending over many years. The scene in their bedroom, as they talk together before slumber, while the old Judge winds up his watch, is a veritable triumph of Art.

The younger daughter Lottie is a vivid portrait of the typical American high-school girl, slangy, superficial, flirtatious, not quite vulgar, and in every emergency with young men fully capable of taking care of herself. After a round of joyous, heart-free, and innocent familiarities with various youthful admirers, she finally becomes an admirable wife and housekeeper. Her sister Ellen is of an opposite temperament, pale, slight, and non-athletic. She is entirely different from the Booth Tarkington or Richard Harding Davis heroine, and in her purity, delicacy, and refinement, takes us back to old-fashioned fiction. As a spectator on the steamer says of her, "that pale girl is adorable." In her shyness and extraordinary loveliness she reminds us of Turgenev's spiritual Lisa. The scene in the night, where her young brother steals to her bed and pours into her sympathetic ears all the troubled passion and sorrow, all the embarrassment and suffering of his sensitive boy's heart, is exceedingly beautiful and tender. He knows *she* will understand. And at last it is Ellen, and not Lottie, who becomes the fashionable, aristocratic, New York woman — preserving in her wealthy environment all the fruits of the spirit.

Boyne, the small boy, the "kid brother," is a fine illustration of the enthusiasm for humanity so characteristic of Mr. Howells. It is instructive to compare this little man with the young brother of Daisy Miller. Both are at the age most trying to their elders, and both are faithfully portrayed; but Randolph C. Miller is made particularly obnoxious, even odious, while one cannot help loving Boyne. The difference is that one is drawn with the finger of scorn and the other with the insight of sympathy. Mr. Howells calls Boyne "a mass of helpless sweetness though he did not know it." His romantic love for the young queen of Holland and the burning mortification he suffers thereby, are sufficiently easy to understand. The contrast between the high seriousness with which he takes himself, and the impression he makes on others, is something that every man who looks back will remember. As the novelist puts it, "He thought he was an iceberg when he was merely an ice cream of heroic mould."

The Kentons, like some other novels by Mr. Howells, may seem to many readers superficial, because it is so largely taken up with the trivial details of daily existence. It is really a profound study of life, made by an artist who has not only the wisdom of the head, but the deeper wisdom of the heart.

IV

BJÖRNSTJERNE BJÖRNSON

FOR over half a century this intellectual athlete has been one of the busiest men in the world. A partisan fighter born and bred, he has been active in every political Skandinavian struggle; in religious questions he has fought first on one side and then on the other, changing only by honest conviction, and hitting with all his might every time; to him the word " education " is as a red rag to a bull, for he believes that it has been mainly bad, and if people will only listen, he can make it mainly good; in a passion of chivalry, he has drawn his pen for the cause of Woman, whose "sphere" he hopes to change — the most modern and the most popular of all the vain attempts to square the circle; his powerful voice has been heard on the lecture platform, not only in his own beloved country, but all over Europe and in America; he has served for years as Theatre-Director, in the determination to convert the playhouse, like everything else he touches, into a vast moral force. In addition to all the excitement of a life spent in fighting, his purely literary activity has been enormous in quantity and astonishing in range. His numerous dramas treat of all possible themes, from the old Sagas to modern divorce laws; and after exhausting all earthly material, he has boldly advanced into the realm of the supernatural; his splendid play, *Beyond Human Power*, holds the boards in most European cities, and has exercised a profound influence on modern drama. His novels are as different in style and purpose as it is possible for the novels of one man to be; and some of them are already classics. A man with such an endowment, with such tremendous convictions, with buoyant optimism and terrific energy, has made no small stir in the world, and it will be a long time before the name of Björnstjerne Björnson is forgotten.

Had he not possessed, in addition to a fine mind, a magnificent physical frame, he would long since have vanished into that spiritual world that has interested him so deeply. But he has the physique of a Norse god. Many instances of his bodily strength and endurance have been cited; it is sufficient to remember that even after his mane of hair had become entirely grey he regularly took his bath by standing naked under a mountain waterfall. Let that suffice, as one trial of it would for most of us. He came honestly by his health and vigour, born as he was on a lonely mountain-side in Norway.

It was in the winter of 1832 that this sturdy baby gave his first cry for freedom, his father being a village pastor, whose flock were literally scattered among steep and desolate rocks, where the salient feature of the landscape during nine months of the year was snow. More than once the good shepherd had to seek and save that which was lost. For society, the little boy had a few pet animals and the dreams engendered by supreme loneliness. But when he was six years old, the father was fortunately called to a pastorate in a beautiful valley on the west coast, surrounded by noble and inspiring scenery, the effect of which is visibly seen in all his early stories. We cannot help comparing this vale of beauty, trailing clouds of glory over Björnson's boyhood, with the flat, wet, dismal gloom of East Prussia, that oppressed so heavily the child Sudermann, and made Dame Care look so grey.

At the grammar school, at the high school, and at the university he showed little interest in the curriculum, and no particular aptitude for study; but before leaving college he had already begun original composition, and at the age of twenty-four he published a masterpiece. This was the pastoral romance, *Synnövé Solbakken*, which for sheer beauty of style and atmosphere he has never surpassed. For some years preceding the date of its appearance there had been a lull in literary activity in Norway.

Out of this premonitory hush of stillness came a beautiful voice, which by the newness and freshness of its tones aroused immediate interest. Everybody listened, enchanted by the strange harmony. Men saw that a new prophet had arisen in Israel. The absolute simplicity of the style, the naïveté of the story, the naturalness of the characters, the short, passionate sentences like those of the Sagas, the lyrically poetic atmosphere, appealed at once to the Norwegian heart. Why is it that we are surprised in books and in plays by simple language and natural characters? It must be that we are so accustomed to literary conventions remote from actual life, that when we behold real people and hear natural talk in works of art our first emotion is glad astonishment. For the same reason we praise certain persons for displaying what we call common sense. Be this as it may, no one believed that a pastoral romance could be so vigorous, so fresh, and so true. Of all forms of literature, pastoral tales, whether in verse or in prose, have been commonly the most artificial and the most insipid; but here was the breath of life. I can recommend nothing better for the soul weary of the closeness of modern naturalism than a course of reading in the early work of Björnson.

He followed this initial success with three other beautiful prose lyrics — *Arne*, *A Happy Boy*, and *The Fisher Maiden*. These stories exhibit the same

qualities so strikingly displayed in *Synnöve Solbakken*.
In all this artistic production Björnson is an impres-
sionist, reproducing with absolute fidelity what he
saw, both in the world of matter and of spirit. We
may rely faithfully on the correctness of these pictures,
whether they portray natural scenery, country customs, or peasant character. We inhale Norway. We
can smell the pines. The nipping and eager air, the
dark green resinous forests — we feel these as
plainly as if we were physically present in the Land
of the Midnight Sun. The kindly simplicity of the
peasants, the village ceremonies at weddings and
funerals, the cheerful loneliness with sheep on
mountain pasture, and the subdued but universal
note of deep rural piety, make one feel as though
the whole community were bound by gold chains
about the feet of God. Björnson says, "The church
is in the foreground of Norwegian peasant life."
And indeed everything seems to centre around
God's acre, and the spire of the meeting-house
points in the same direction as the stories themselves.
Many beautiful passages affect us like noble music;
our eyes are filled with happy tears.

In view of the strong and ardent personality of
the author, it is curious that these early romances
should be so truly objective. One feels his personality in a general way, as one feels that of Turgenev;
but the young writer separates himself entirely from

the course of the story; he nowhere interferes. The characters apparently develop without his assistance, as the events take place without any manipulation. As a work of objective art, *Synnöve Solbakken* approaches flawless perfection. It has one plot, which travels in one direction — forward. The persons are intensely Norwegian, but there their similarity ends. Each is individualised. The simplicity of the story is so remarkable that to some superficial and unobservant readers it has seemed childish. The very acme of Art is so close to nature that it sometimes is mistaken for no art at all, like the acting of Garrick or the style of Jane Austen. Adverse criticisms are the highest compliments. Language is well managed when it expresses profound thoughts in words clear to a child.

The love scenes in this narrative are idyllic; in fact, the whole book is an idyl. It seems radiant with sunshine. It is as pure as a mountain lake, and as refreshing. And besides the artistic unity of the work, that satisfies one's standards so fully, there is an exquisite something hard to define; a play of fancy, a veil of poetic beauty lingering over the story, that makes us feel when we have closed the book as if we were gazing at a clear winter sunset.

Björnson has the creative imagination of the true poet. In the wonderful prologue to *Arne* he gives the trees separate personalities, in a manner to arouse almost the envy of Thomas Hardy. Indeed, the author of *The Woodlanders* has never felt the trees more intensely than the Norwegian novelist. The prose style unconsciously breaks into verse form at times, with the natural grace and ease of a singing bird. Not the least charming incidents in Björnson's romances are the frequent lyrics, that spring up like cowslips in a pasture.

"Punctual as Springtide forth peep they."

* * * * * * * *

The novels in Björnson's second period are so totally unlike those we have just been considering that if all his work had been published anonymously, no one would have ventured to say that the same man had written *A Happy Boy* and *In God's Way*. There came a pause in his creative activity. He wrote little imaginative literature, and many thought the well of his inspiration had gone dry. Really he was passing through a belated *Sturm und Drang;* a tremendous intellectual struggle and fermentation had set in, from which he emerged mentally a changed man, with a new outfit of opinions and ideas. At nearly the same time his great contemporary Tolstoi was also in the Slough of Despond, but he climbed out on the other side and set his face towards the Celestial City. Björnson's floundering ultimately carried him in precisely the opposite direction. While Tolstoi was studying the New Testament, Björnson applied himself to Darwin, Mill, and Spencer, and became completely converted from the Christianity of his youth. Many minds would have been temporarily paralysed by such a result, and would finally have become either pessimistic or coldly critical. But Björnson simply could not endure to be a gloomy, cynical spectator of life, like his countryman, Ibsen, any more than he could leave his native land and calmly view its nakedness from the comfortable environment of Munich or Rome. Björnson has the sort of intellect that cannot remain in equilibrium. He was ever a fighter, and cannot live without something to fight for. The natural optimism of his temperament, so opposed in every way to the blank despair of Ibsen, made him see in his new views the way of salvation. He is just as sure he is right now as he was when he held opinions exactly the contrary. With joyful ardour he became the champion and propagandist of democracy in politics and of free thought in religion; apparently adopting Spencer's saying, "To the true reformer no institution is sacred, no belief above criticism." For the word "reformer" precisely describes Björnson; like the chief characters in his later novels, he is an apostle of reform, zealous, tireless, and tiresome.

Lowell, in his fine essay on Gray, said that one reason why the eighteenth century was so comfortable was that "responsibility for the universe had not yet been invented." Now Björnson feels this responsibility with all the strength of his nature, and however admirable it may be as a moral quality, it has vitiated his artistic career. As he renounced Christianity for agnosticism, so he renounced romance for realism. The novels written since 1875 are not only unlike his early pastoral romances in literary style; they are totally different productions in tone, in spirit, and in intention. And, from the point of view of art, they are, in my opinion, as inferior to the work of his youth as Hawthorne's campaign *Life of Pierce* is inferior to *The Scarlet Letter*. In every way Björnson is farther off from heaven than when he was a boy.

In addition to many short sketches, his later period includes three realistic novels. These are: *Flags Are Flying in Town and Harbour*, translated into English with the title, *The Heritage of the Kurts*, for it is a study in heredity; *In God's Way*,[1] loudly proclaimed as his masterpiece, and *Mary*. The first two originally attracted more attention abroad than at home. The *Flags* hung idly in Norway, and the orthodox were not anxious to get in God's way. But the second book

[1] In the original the title is "In God's Ways."

produced considerable excitement in England, which finally reacted in Christiania and Copenhagen; it is still hotly discussed. In these three novels the author has stepped out of the rôle of artist and become a kind of professor of pedagogy, his speciality being the education of women. In *Flags* the principal part of the story is taken up with a girls' school, which gives the novelist an opportunity to include a confused study of heredity, and to air all sorts of educational theory. The chief one appears to be that in the curriculum for young girls the "major" should be physiology. Hygiene, which so many bewildered persons are accepting just now in lieu of the Gospel, plays a heavy part in Björnson's later work. The gymnasium in *Flags* takes the place of the church in *Synnöve;* and acrobatic feats of the body are deemed more healthful than the religious aspirations of the soul. Kallem, a prominent character of the story *In God's Way*, usually appears walking on his hands, which is not the only fashion in which he is upside down. The book *Flags* is, frankly speaking, an intolerable bore. The hero, Rendalen, who also appears in the subsequent novel, is the mouthpiece of the new opinions of the author; a convenient if clumsy device, for whenever Björnson wishes to expound his views on education, hygiene, or religion, he simply makes Rendalen deliver a lecture. Didactic novels are in general a poor substitute either for learning or for fiction, but they are doubly bad when the author is confused in his ideas of science and in his notions of art. One general "lesson" emerges from the jargon of this book — that men should suffer for immorality as severely as women, a doctrine neither new nor practicable. The difficulty is that with Björnson, as with some others who shout this edict, the equalising of the punishment takes the form of leaving the men as they are, and issuing a general pardon to the women. Rendalen, the head-master of the school, is constantly bringing up this topic, and he makes it the chief subject for discussion in the girls' debating society! These females are going to be emancipated. A pseudo-scientific twist is also given to this novel by the introduction of mesmerism and hypnotic influence, matters in which the author is deeply interested. We are given to understand that a large number of women are annually ruined, not by their lack of moral conviction and will power, but simply by the hypnotic influence of men. One may perhaps reasonably doubt the ultimate value of a wide dissemination of this great idea, especially in a young ladies' seminary. To the unsympathetic reader, the one question that will keep him afloat in all this welter, is not concerned with pedagogy; it is the honest attempt to discover why the book bears its strange title. Unfortunately he will not find out until the last leaf. Then

"the connexion of which with the plot one sees."

It is pleasant to take up the volume *In God's Way*, for, however disappointing it may be to those who know the young Björnson, it is vastly superior to *Flags*. It is what is called to-day a "strong" novel, and has naturally evoked the widest variation of comment. By many it has been greeted with enthusiastic admiration and by many with outspoken disgust. Psychologically, it is indeed powerful. The characters are interesting, and they develop in a way that may or may not be God's, but resemble His in being mysterious. One cannot foresee in the early chapters what is going to happen to the *dramatis personæ*, nor what is to be our final attitude toward any of them. Think of the impression made on us by our first acquaintance with Josephine, or Kallem, or Ragni, or Ole; and then compare it with the state of our feelings as we draw near the end. Not one of these characters remains the same; each one develops, and develops as he might in actual life. Björnson does not approach his men and women from an easy chair, in the descriptive manner; once created, we feel that they would grow without his aid.

For all this particular triumph of art, *In God's*

Way is plainly a didactic novel, with the author preaching from beginning to end. The "fighting" quality in the novelist gets the better of his literary genius. We have a story in the extreme realistic style, marked by occasional scenes of great beauty and force; but the exposition of doctrine is somewhat vague and confused, and the construction of the whole work decidedly inartistic. Two general points, however, are made clear: First, that one may walk in God's way without believing in God. Religion is of no importance in comparison with conduct, nor have the two things any vital or necessary connexion. This is a modern view, and perhaps a natural reaction from the strictness of Björnson's childhood training. Second, that virtue is a matter entirely of the heart, bearing no relation whatever to the statute-book. A woman may be legally an adulteress and yet absolutely pure. This also is quite familiar to us in the pages of modern dramatists and novelists. Björnson has taken an extraordinary instance to prove his thesis, a thesis that perhaps needs no emphasis, for human nature is only too well disposed to make its moral creed coincide with its bodily instincts.

The same theme — mental as opposed to physical female chastity — is the leading idea of *Mary*, a novel that has had considerable success in Norway and in Germany, but has only this year been translated into English. This work of his old age shows not the slightest trace of decay. It is an interesting and powerful analysis of a girl's heart, written in short, vigorous sentences. Mary, after taking plenty of time for reflexion, and without any solicitation, deliberately gives herself to her lover, in a manner exactly similar to a scene in Maupassant's novel, *Notre Cœur*. Her fiancé is naturally amazed, as there has been nothing leading up to this; she comes to him of her own free will. Her theory of conduct (which exemplifies that of Björnson) is that a woman is the sovereign mistress of her own body, and can do what she pleases. There is nothing immoral in a woman's free gift of herself to her lover, provided she does it out of her royal bounty, and not as a weak yielding to masculine pursuit. The next day Mary is grievously disappointed to discover that, instead of the homage and worship she expected, the erstwhile timid lover glories in the sense of possession. She fears that she cannot live an absolutely independent life with such a husband — and Björnson's gospel is, of course, the untrammelled freedom of woman. So, although she is about to become a mother, she deliberately cancels the engagement to the putative child's father; this puzzles him even more than her previous conduct, though he is forced to acquiesce. Then, in a final access of despair, as she is about to commit suicide, she is rescued by a man whose love is like the moth's for the star — who tells her that no matter what she has done, she is the noblest, purest woman on earth, and the chaste queen of his heart. Thus, by a stroke of good fortune, rather than by anything inevitable in the story, the book ends happily, with Mary and her second adoring lover in the very delirium of joy. It is evident that the novel is nothing but a *Tendenz-Roman;* Björnson wishes us to approve of his heroine's conduct throughout — of the entirely unnecessary sacrifice of her virtue, of the subsequent sacrifice of her reputation, and of her remorseless joy in the arms of another man. Such is to be the doctrine of sex equality; men are not to be made more virtuous, but the freedom of women is not only to be pardoned, but approved.

In comparing the three late with the four early novels, the most striking change is instantly apparent to anyone who reads *Synnövé Solbakken* and then opens *In God's Way.* It is the sudden and depressing change of air, from the mountains to the sickroom. The abundance of medical detail in the later novel is almost nauseating, and would be wholly so were it not absurd. One has only to compare the invigorating scenery and the simple love scenes in *Synnövé* with the minute examination of Ragni's spittle (for tuberculosis) in the other book — but enough is said. Despite all that has been written in praise of Björnson's "courage" in dealing with problems of sex and disease, I sympathise with the cry of his friend in 1879: —

"Come back again, dear Björnson, come back!"

It is easy to see that the influence of modern English scepticism cannot account entirely for the revolution in the Norwegian's mind and art. We can clearly observe an attraction much nearer, that has drawn this luminous star so far out of its course. It is none other than the mighty Ibsen. Ibsen's analysis of disease, his examination of marriage problems, his Ishmaelite attacks on the present structure of civilised society — all this has had its effect on his contemporary and countryman. As a destructive force Ibsen was stronger than Björnson, because he was ruthless. But one had the courage of despair, while the other has the courage of hope. Björnson does not believe in Fate and is not afraid of it. He loves and believes in humanity. His gloomiest books end with a vision. There is always a rift in the clouds. Throughout all his career he has set his face steadfastly toward what he has taken to be the true light. Such men compel admiration, no matter whose colours they bear. And however much we may deplore his present course, we cannot now echo the cry of his friend and say, "Come back!" The language of the poet better expresses our attitude: —

"Life's night begins: let him never come back to us!
  There would be doubt, hesitation, and pain,
  Forced praise on our part — the glimmer of twilight,
  Never glad confident morning again!
  Best fight on well, for we taught him — strike gallantly,
  Menace our heart ere we master his own;
  Then let him receive the new knowledge and wait us,
  Pardoned in heaven, the first by the throne!"

V

MARK TWAIN

During the last twenty years, a profound change has taken place in the attitude of the reading public toward Mark Twain. I can remember very well when he was regarded merely as a humorist, and one opened his books with an anticipatory grin. Very few supposed that he belonged to literature; and a complete, uniform edition of his *Works* would perhaps have been received with something of the mockery that greeted Ben Jonson's folio in 1616. Professor Richardson's *American Literature*, which is still a standard work, appeared originally in 1886. My copy, which bears the date 1892, contains only two references in the index to Mark Twain, while Mr. Cable, for example, receives ten; and the whole volume fills exactly nine hundred and ninety pages. Looking up one of the two references, we find the following opinion: —

"But there is a class of writers, authors ranking below Irving or Lowell, and lacking the higher artistic or moral purpose of the greater humorists, who amuse a generation and then pass from sight. Every period demands a new manner of jest, after the current fashion. . . . The reigning favourites of the day are Frank R. Stockton, Joel Chandler Harris, the various newspaper jokers, and 'Mark Twain.' But the creators of 'Pomona' and 'Rudder Grange,' of 'Uncle Remus and his Folk-lore Stories,' and 'Innocents Abroad,' clever as they are, must make hay while the sun shines. Twenty years hence, unless they chance to enshrine their wit in some higher literary achievement, their unknown successors will be the privileged comedians of the republic. Humour alone never gives its masters a place in literature; it must coexist with literary qualities, and must usually be joined with such pathos as one finds in Lamb, Hood, Irving, or Holmes."

It is interesting to remember that before this pronouncement was published, *Tom Sawyer* and *Huckleberry Finn* had been read by thousands. Professor Richardson continued: "Two or three divisions of American humour deserve somewhat more respectful treatment," and he proceeds to give a full page to Petroleum V. Nasby, another page to Artemus Ward, and two and one-half pages to Josh Billings, while Mark Twain had received less than four lines. After stating that, in the case of authors like Mark Twain, "temporary amusement, not literary product, is the thing sought and given," Professor Richardson announces that the department of fiction will be considered later. In this "department," Mark Twain is not mentioned at all, although Julian Hawthorne receives over three pages!

I have quoted Professor Richardson at length, because he is a deservedly high authority, and well represents an attitude toward Mark Twain that was common all during the eighties. Another college professor, who is to-day one of the best living American critics, says, in his *Initial Studies in American Letters* (1895), "Though it would be ridiculous to maintain that either of these writers [Artemus Ward and Mark Twain] takes rank with Lowell and Holmes, . . . still it will not do to ignore them as mere buffoons, or even to predict that their humours will soon be forgotten." There is no allusion in his book to *Tom Sawyer* or *Huckleberry Finn*, nor does the critic seem to regard their creator as in any sense a novelist. Still another writer, in a passing allusion to Mark Twain, says, "Only a very small portion of his writing has any place as literature."

Literary opinions change as time progresses; and no one could have observed the remarkable demonstration at the seventieth birthday of our great national humorist without feeling that most of his contemporaries regarded him, not as their peer, but as their Chief. Without wishing to make any invidious comparisons, I cannot refrain from commenting on the statement that it would be "ridiculous" to maintain that Mark Twain takes rank with Oliver Wendell Holmes. It is, of course, absolutely impossible to predict the future; the only real test of the value of a book is Time. Who now reads Cowley? Time has laughed at so many contemporary judgements that it would be fool-hardy to make positive assertions about literary stock quotations one hundred years from now. Still, guesses are not prohibited; and I think it not unlikely that the name of Mark Twain will out-last the name of Holmes. American Literature would surely be the poorer if the great Boston Brahmin had not enlivened it with his rich humour, his lambent wit, and his sincere pathos; but the whole content of his work seems slighter than the big American prose epics of the man of our day.

Indeed, it seems to me that Mark Twain is our foremost living American writer. He has not the subtlety of Henry James or the wonderful charm of Mr. Howells; he could not have written *Daisy Miller*, or *A Modern Instance*, or *Indian Summer*, or *The Kentons* — books which exhibit literary quality of an exceedingly high order. I have read them over and over again, with constantly increas-ing profit and delight. I wish that Mr. Howells might live for ever, and give to every generation the pure intellectual joy that he has given to ours. But the natural endowment of Mark Twain is still greater. Mr. Howells has made the most of him-self; God has done it all for Mark Twain. If there be a living American writer touched with true genius, whose books glow with the divine fire, it is he. He has always been a conscientious artist; but no amount of industry could ever have produced a *Huckleberry Finn*.

When I was a child at the West Middle Grammar School of Hartford, on one memorable April day, Mark Twain addressed the graduating-class. I was thirteen years old, but I have found it impossible to forget what he said. The subject of his "remarks" was Methuselah. He informed us that Methuselah lived to the ripe old age of nine hundred and sixty-nine. But he might as well have lived to be several thousand — nothing happened. The speaker told us that we should all live longer than Methuselah. Fifty years of Europe are better than a cycle of Cathay, and twenty years of modern American life are longer and richer in content than the old patriarch's thousand. Ours will be the true age in which to live, when more will happen in a day than in a year of the flat existence of our ancestors. I cannot remember his words; but what a fine thing it is to hear a speech, and carry away an idea!

I have since observed that this idea runs through much of his literary work. His philosophy of life underlies his broadest burlesque — for *A Connecticut Yankee in King Arthur's Court* is simply an exposure of the "good old times." Mark Twain believes in the Present, in human progress. Too often do we apprehend the Middle Ages through the glowing pages of Spenser and Walter Scott; we see only glittering processions of ladies dead and lovely knights. Mark Twain shows us the wretched condition of the common people, their utter ignorance and degradation, the coarseness and immorality of technical chivalry, the cruel and unscrupulous ecclesiastical tyranny, and the capricious insolence of the barons. One may regret that he has reversed the dynamics in so glorious a book as Malory's *Morte d'Arthur*, but, through all the buffoonery and roaring mirth with which the knights in armour are buried, the artistic and moral purpose of the satirist is clear. If I understand him rightly, he would have us believe that *our* age, not theirs, is the "good time"; nay, ours is the age of magic and wonder. We need not regret in melancholy sentimentality the picturesqueness of bygone days, for we ourselves live, not in a material and commonplace generation, but in the very midst of miracles and romance. Merlin and the Fay Morgana would have given all their petty skill to have been able to use a telephone or a phonograph, or to see a moving picture. The sleeping princess and her castle were awakened by a kiss; but in the twentieth century a man in Washington touches a button, and hundreds of miles away tons of machinery begin to move, fountains begin to play, and the air resounds with the whir of wheels. In comparison with to-day, the age of chivalry seems dull and poor. Even in chivalry itself our author is more knightly than Lancelot; for was there ever a more truly chivalrous performance than Mark Twain's essay on Harriet Shelley, or his literary monument to Joan of Arc? In these earnest pages, our national humorist appears as the true knight.

Mark Twain's humour is purely American. It is not the humour of Washington Irving, which resembles that of Addison and Thackeray; it is not delicate and indirect. It is genial, sometimes outrageous, mirth — laughter holding both his sides. I have found it difficult to read him in a library or on a street-car, for explosions of pent-up mirth or a distorted face are apt to attract unpleasant attention in such public places. Mark Twain's humour is boisterous, uproarious, colossal, overwhelming. As has often been remarked, the Americans are not naturally a gay people, like the French; nor are we light-hearted and careless, like the Irish and the Negro. At heart, we are intensely serious, nervous, melancholy. For humour, therefore, we naturally turn to buffoonery and burlesque, as a reaction against the strain and tension of life. Our attitude is something like that of the lonely author of the *Anatomy of Melancholy,* who used to lean over the parapet of Magdalen Bridge, and shake with mirth at the obscene jokes of the bargemen. We like Mark Twain's humour, not because we are frivolous, but because we are just the reverse. I have never known a frivolous person who really enjoyed or appreciated Mark Twain.

The essence of Mark Twain's humour is Incongruity. The jumping frog is named Daniel Webster; and, indeed, the intense gravity of a frog's face, with the droop at the corners of the mouth, might well be envied by many an American Senator. When the shotted frog vainly attempted to leave the earth, he shrugged his shoulders "like a Frenchman." Bilgewater and the Dolphin on the raft are grotesquely incongruous figures. The rescuing of Jim from his prison cell is full of the most incongruous ideas, his common-sense attitude toward the whole transaction contrasting strangely with that of the romantic Tom. Along with the constant incongruity goes the element of surprise — which Professor Beers has well pointed out. When one begins a sentence, in an apparently serious discussion, one never knows how it will end. In discussing the peace that accompanies religious faith, Mark Twain says that he has often been impressed with the calm confidence of a Christian with four aces. Exaggeration — deliberate, enormous hyperbole — is another feature. Rudyard Kipling, who

has been profoundly influenced by Mark Twain,
and has learned much from him, often employs
the same device, as in *Brugglesmith*. Irreverence
is also a noteworthy quality. In his travel-books,
we are given the attitude of the typical American
Philistine toward the wonders and sacred relics of
the Old World, the whole thing being a gigantic
burlesque on the sentimental guide-books which
were so much in vogue before the era of Baedeker.
With such continuous fun and mirth, satire and
burlesque, it is no wonder that Mark Twain should
not always be at his best. He is doubtless sometimes flat, sometimes coarse, as all humorists since
Rabelais have been. The wonder is that his level
has been so high. I remember, just before the
appearance of *Following the Equator*, I had been
told that Mark Twain's inspiration was finally
gone, and that he could not be funny if he tried.
To test this, I opened the new book, and this is
what I found on the first page: —

"We sailed for America, and there made certain prepara-
tions. This took but little time. Two members of my
family elected to go with me. Also a carbuncle. The dictionary says a carbuncle is a kind of jewel. Humour is out
of place in a dictionary."

Although Mark Twain has the great qualities of
the true humorist — common sense, human sympathy, and an accurate eye for proportion — he is

much more than a humorist. His work shows
high literary quality, the quality that appears in
first-rate novels. He has shown himself to be a
genuine artist. He has done something which
many popular novelists have signally failed to accomplish — he has created real characters. His
two wonderful boys, Tom Sawyer and Huckleberry
Finn, are wonderful in quite different ways. The
creator of Tom exhibited remarkable observation;
the creator of Huck showed the divine touch of
imagination. Tom is the American boy — he is
"smart." In having his fence whitewashed, in
controlling a pool of Sabbath-school tickets at the
precise psychological moment, he displays abundant
promise of future success in business. Huck, on
the other hand, is the child of nature, harmless, sincere, and crudely imaginative. His reasonings with
Jim about nature and God belong to the same
department of natural theology as that illustrated
in Browning's *Caliban*. The night on the raft with
Jim, when these two creatures look aloft at the stars,
and Jim reckons the moon *laid* them, is a case in
point.

"We had the sky up there, all speckled with stars, and we
used to lay on our backs and look up at them, and discuss
about whether they was made or just happened. Jim he
allowed they was made, but I allowed they happened; I
judged it would have took too long to *make* so many. Jim
said the moon could a *laid* them; well, that looked kind

of reasonable, so I didn't say nothing against it, because I've seen a frog lay most as many, so of course it could be done. We used to watch the stars that fell, too, and see them streak down. Jim allowed they'd got spoiled and was hove out of the nest."

Again, Mark Twain has so much dramatic power that, were his literary career beginning instead of closing, he might write for us the great American play that we are still awaiting. The story of the feud between the Grangerfords and the Shepherdsons is thrillingly dramatic, and the tragic climax seizes the heart. The shooting of the drunken Boggs, the gathering of the mob, and its control by one masterful personality, belong essentially to true drama, and are written with power and insight. The pathos of these scenes is never false, never mawkish or overdone; it is the pathos of life itself. Mark Twain's extraordinary skill in descriptive passages shows, not merely keen observation, but the instinct for the specific word — the one word that is always better than any of its synonyms, for it makes the picture real — it creates the illusion, which is the essence of all literary art. The storm, for example: —

"It was my watch below till twelve, but I wouldn't a turned in anyway if I'd had a bed, because a body don't see such a storm as that every day in the week, not by a long sight. My souls, how the wind did scream along! And every second or two there'd come a glare that lit up the white-caps for a

half a mile around, and you'd see the islands looking dusty
through the rain, and the trees thrashing around in the wind;
then comes a *h-wach!* — bum! bum! bumble-umble-um-
bum-bum-bum-bum — and the thunder would go rumbling
and grumbling away, and quit — and then *rip* comes another
flash and another sockdolager. The waves 'most washed
me off the raft sometimes, but I hadn't any clothes on, and
didn't mind. We didn't have no trouble about snags; the
lightning was glaring and flittering around so constant that
we could see them plenty soon enough to throw her head this
way or that and miss them."

Tom Sawyer and *Huckleberry Finn* are prose
epics of American life. The former is one of those
books — of which *The Pilgrim's Progress, Gulliver's
Travels*, and *Robinson Crusoe* are supreme examples
— that are read at different periods of one's life
from very different points of view; so that it is not
easy to say when one enjoys them the most — before
one understands their real significance or after.
Nearly all healthy boys enjoy reading *Tom Sawyer*,
because the intrinsic interest of the story is so great,
and the various adventures of the hero are portrayed
with such gusto. Yet it is impossible to outgrow
the book. The eternal Boy is there, and one cannot appreciate the nature of boyhood properly until
one has ceased to be a boy. The other masterpiece,
Huckleberry Finn, is really not a child's book at all.
Children devour it, but they do not digest it. It
is a permanent picture of a certain period of Ameri-

can history, and this picture is made complete, not so much by the striking portraits of individuals placed on the huge canvas, as by the vital unity of the whole composition. If one wishes to know what life on the Mississippi really was, to know and understand the peculiar social conditions of that highly exciting time, one has merely to read through this powerful narrative, and a definite, coherent, vivid impression remains.

By those who have lived there, and whose minds are comparatively free from prejudice, Mark Twain's pictures of life in the South before the war are regarded as, on the whole, nearer the truth than those supplied by any other artist. One reason for this is the aim of the author; he was not trying to support or to defend any particular theory — no, his aim was purely and wholly artistic. In *Uncle Tom's Cabin*, a book by no means devoid of literary art, the red-hot indignation of the author largely nullified her evident desire to tell the truth. If one succeeds in telling the truth about anything whatever, one must have something more than the *desire* to tell the truth; one must know how to do it. False impressions do not always, probably do not commonly, come from deliberate liars. Mrs. Stowe's astonishing work is not really the history of slavery; it is the history of abolition sentiment. On the other hand, writers so graceful, talented, and clever as Mr. Page and Mr. Hopkinson Smith do not always give us pictures that correctly represent, except locally, the actual situation before the war; for these gentlemen seem to have *Uncle Tom's Cabin* in mind. Mark Twain gives us both points of view; he shows us the beautiful side of slavery, — for it had a wonderfully beautiful, patriarchal side, — and he also shows us the horror of it. The living dread of the Negro that he would be sold down the river, has never been more vividly represented than when the poor woman in *Pudd'nhead Wilson* sees the water swirling against the snag, and realises that she is bound the wrong way. That one scene makes an indelible impression on the reader's mind, and counteracts tons of polemics. The peculiar harmlessness of Jim is beautiful to contemplate. Although he and Huck really own the raft, and have taken all the risk, they obey implicitly the orders of the two tramps who call themselves Duke and King. Had that been a raft on the Connecticut River, and had Huck and Jim been Yankees, they would have said to the intruders, "Whose raft is this, anyway?"

Mark Twain may be trusted to tell the truth; for the eye of the born caricature artist always sees the salient point. Caricatures often give us a better idea of their object than a photograph; for the things that are exaggerated, be it a large nose, or a long neck, are, after all, the things that differentiate this particular individual from the mass. Everybody remembers how Tweed was caught by one of Nast's cartoons.

Mark Twain is through and through American. If foreigners really wish to know the American spirit, let them read Mark Twain. He is far more American than their favourite specimen, Walt Whitman. The essentially American qualities of common sense, energy, enterprise, good-humour, and Philistinism fairly shriek from his pages. He reveals us in our limitations, in our lack of appreciation of certain beautiful things, fully as well as he pictures us in coarser but more triumphant aspects. It is, of course, preposterous to say that Americans are totally different from other humans; we have no monopoly of common sense and good-humour, nor are we all hide-bound Philistines. But there is something pronounced in the American character, and the books of Mark Twain reveal it. He has also more than once been a valuable and efficient champion. Without being an offensive and blatant Jingo, I think he is content to be an American.

Mark Twain is our great Democrat. Democracy is his political, social, and moral creed. His hatred of snobbery, affectation, and assumed superiority is total. His democracy has no limits; it is bottomless and far-reaching. Nothing seems really sacred to him except the sacred right of every individual to do exactly as he pleases; which means, of course, that no one can interfere with another's right, for then democracy would be the privilege of a few, and would stultify itself. Not only does the spirit of democracy breathe out from all his greater books, but it is shown in specific instances, such as *Travelling with a Reformer;* and Mark Twain has more than once given testimony for his creed, without recourse to the pen.

At the head of all American novelists, living and dead, stands Nathaniel Hawthorne, unapproached, possibly unapproachable. His fine and subtle art is an altogether different thing from the art of our mighty, democratic, national humorist. But Literature is wonderfully diverse in its content; and the historian of American Letters, in the far future, will probably find it impossible to omit the name of Mark Twain.

VI

HENRYK SIENKIEWICZ

In a private letter to a friend, written in 1896, the late Mr. Charles Dudley Warner remarked: "I am just reading *Children of the Soil*, which I got in London before I sailed. It confirms me in my very high opinion of him. I said the other day that I think him at the head of living novelists, both in range, grasp of a historical situation, intuition and knowledge of human nature. Comparisons are always dangerous, but I know no historical novelist who is his superior, or who is more successful in creating characters. His canvas is very large, and in the beginning of his historical romances the reader needs patience, but the picture finally comes out vividly, and the episodes in the grand story are perfectly enthralling. Of his novels of modern life I cannot speak too highly. The subtlety of his analysis is wonderful, and the shades of character are delineated by slight but always telling strokes. There is the same reality in them that is in his romances. As to the secret of his power, who can say? It is genius (I still believe in that word) but re-enforced by very hard labour and study, by much reading, and by acute observation."

This letter may serve as an excellent summary of the opinions of many intelligent American critics concerning a writer whose name was unknown to us in 1890, and of whom the whole world was talking in 1895.[1] One reason — apart from their intrinsic excellence — for the Byronic suddenness of the fame of the Polish Trilogy, was the psychological opportuneness of its appearance. In England and in America the recent Romantic Revival was at its flood; we were all reading historical romances, and were hungry for more. Sienkiewicz satisfied us by providing exactly what we were looking for. In his own country he was idolised, for his single pen had done more than many years of tumultuous discussion, to put Poland back on the map of Europe. At the exercises commemorating the five hundredth anniversary of the University of Cracow, the late President Gilman, who had the well-deserved honour of speaking for the universities of America, said: "America thanks Poland for three great names: Copernicus, to whom all the world is indebted; Kosciuszko, who spilled his blood for American independence; and Sienkiewicz, whose name is

---

[1] His name does not appear in standard English biographical dictionaries or literary reference books for 1893 or 1894.

a household word in thousands of American homes, and who has introduced Poland to the American people."[1]

Sienkiewicz was born in 1845. After student days at Warsaw, he came over in 1876–1877 to California, in a party that included Madame Modjeska. They attempted to establish a kind of socialistic community, which bears in the retrospect a certain resemblance to Brook Farm. Fortunately for the cause of art, which the world needs more than it does socialism, the enterprise was a failure. Sienkiewicz returned to Poland, and began his literary career; Madame Modjeska became one of the chief ornaments of the English stage for a quarter of a century. Her ashes now rest in the ancient Polish city where President Gilman uttered his fine tribute to the friend of her youth.

The three great Polish romances were all written in the eighties; and at about the same time the author was also engaged in the composition of purely realistic work, which displays his powers in a quite different form of art, and constitutes the most original — though not the most popular — part of his literary production. The *Children of the Soil*, which some of the elect in Poland consider his masterpiece, is a novel, constructed and executed in the strictest

[1] See an interesting article in the *Outlook* for 3 August, 1901 *A Visit to Sienkiewicz*, by L. E. Van Norman.

style of realism; *Without Dogma* is still farther removed from the Romantic manner, for it is a story of psychological analytical introspection. Sienkiewicz himself regards *Children of the Soil* as his favourite, although he is "not prepared to say just why." And *Without Dogma* he thinks to be "in many respects my strongest work." It is evident that he does not consider himself primarily a maker of stirring historical romance. But in the nineties he returned to this form of fiction, producing his Roman panorama called *Quo Vadis*, which, although it has made the biggest noise of all his books, is perhaps the least valuable. Like *Ben Hur*, it was warmed over into a tremendously successful melodrama, and received the final compliment of parody.[1] Toward the close of the century, Sienkiewicz completed another massive historical romance, *The Knights of the Cross*, which, in its abundant action, striking characterisation, and charming humour, recalled the Trilogy; this was followed by *On the Field of Glory*, and we may confidently expect more, though never too much; he simply could not be dull if he tried.

In a time like ours, when literary tabloids take the place of wholesome mental food, when many

[1] One of the most grotesque and laughable burlesques ever seen on the American stage was the travesty of *Quo Vadis*, with the heroine Lithia, who drew a lobster on the sand: the strong man, Zero, wrenched the neck off a wild borax.

successful novels can be read at a sitting or a lying
— requiring no exertion either of soul or body —
the portentous size of these Polish stories is a magnificent challenge. If some books are to be tasted,
others to be swallowed, and some few to be chewed
and digested, what shall we do with Sienkiewicz?
In Mr. Curtin's admirable translation, the Trilogy
covers over twenty-five hundred closely printed
pages; the *Knights of the Cross* over seven hundred
and fifty, *Children of the Soil* over six hundred and
fifty; *Without Dogma* (Englished by another hand)
has been silently so much abridged in translation
that we do not know what its actual length may
be. We do not rebel, because the next chapter
is invariably not a task, but a temptation; but when
we wake up with a start at the call *Finis*, which
magic word transfers us from the seventeenth to the
twentieth century, and contemplate the vast fabric
of our dream, we cannot help asking if there is any
law in the construction that requires so much
material. Gogol, in his astonishing romance, *Taras
Bulba*, which every lover of Sienkiewicz should
read, gives us the same impression of Vastness, in
a book Lilliputian in size. Nor is there any apparent reason why the Polish narratives should
stop on the last page, nor indeed stop at all.
Combat succeeds combat, when in the midst of
the hurly-burly, the Master of the Show calls time.

It is his arbitrary will, rather than any inevitable succession of events, that shuts off the scene: the men might be fighting yet. This passion for mere detail mars the first part of *With Fire and Sword;* one cannot see the forest for the trees.

One reason for this immensity is the author's desire to be historically accurate, the besetting sin of many recent dramas and novels. Before beginning to write, Sienkiewicz reads all the authorities and documentary evidence he can find. The result is plainly seen in the early pages of *With Fire and Sword,* which read far more like a history than like a work of fiction — note the striking contrast in *Pan Michael!* The *Knights of the Cross* appeared with maps. The topography of *Quo Vadis* was so carefully prepared that it almost serves as a guide-book to ancient Rome. Now the relation of History to Fiction has never been better stated than by Lessing: "The dramatist uses history, not because it has happened, but because it has so happened that he could scarcely find anything else better adapted to his purpose." No work of fiction has ever gained immortality by its historical accuracy.

Everyone notices that the works of Sienkiewicz are Epics rather than Novels. Even bearing Fielding clearly in mind, there is no better illustration to be found in literary history. The Trilogy bears the same relation to the wars of Poland that the

Iliad bears to the struggle at Troy. The scope and flow of the narrative, the power of the scenes, the vast perspective, the portraits of individual heroes, the impassioned poetry of the style — all these qualities are of the Epic. The intense patriotism is thrilling, and makes one envy the sensations of native readers. And yet the reasons for the downfall of Poland are made perfectly clear.

Is the *romanticist* Sienkiewicz an original writer? In the narrow and strict sense of the word, I think not. He is eclectic rather than original. He is a skilful fuser of material, like Shakespeare. At any rate, his most conspicuous virtue is not originality. He has enormous force, a glorious imagination, astonishing facility, and a remarkable power of making pictures, both in panorama and in miniature; but his work shows constantly the inspiration not only of his historical authorities, but of previous poets and novelists. Those who are really familiar with the writings of Homer, Shakespeare, Scott, and Dumas, will not require further comment on this point. The influence of Homer is seen in the constant similes, the epithets like "incomparable bowman," and the stress laid on the deeds of individual heroes; a thing quite natural in Homeric warfare, but rather disquieting in the days of villainous saltpetre. The three swordsmen in *With Fire and Sword* — Pan Yan, Pan Podbienta, and Pan

Michael — infallibly remind us of Dumas's three guardsmen; and the great duel scenes in the same story, and in the *Knights of the Cross*, are quite in the manner of the Frenchman. Would that other writers could employ their reminiscences to such advantage! In the high colouring, in the management of historical events, and in patriotic enthusiasm, we cannot help thinking of Scott. But be the debt to Dumas and to Scott as great as one pleases to estimate, I am free to acknowledge that I find the romances of the Pole more enthralling than those of either or both of his two great predecessors.

With reference to the much-discussed character of Zagloba, I confess I cannot join in the common verdict that pronounces him a "new creation in literature." Those who believe this delightful person to be something new and original have simply forgotten Falstaff. If one will begin all over again, and read the two parts of *Henry IV*, and then take a look at Zagloba, the author of his being is immediately apparent. Zagloba is a Polish Falstaff, an astonishingly clever imitation of the real thing. He is old, white-haired, fat, a resourceful wit and humorist, better at bottles than at battles, and yet bold when policy requires: in every essential feature of body and mind he resembles the immortal creation of Shakespeare. Sienkiewicz *develops* him with subtle skill and affectionate solicitude, even as

Dickens developed Mr. Pickwick; the Zagloba of *Pan Michael* is far sweeter and more mellow than when we make his acquaintance in the first volume of the Trilogy; but the last word for this character is the word " original." The real triumph of Sienkiewicz in the portrayal of the jester is in the fact that he could imitate Falstaff without spoiling him, for no other living writer could have done it. A copy that can safely be placed alongside the original implies art of a very high class. To see Zagloba is to realise the truth of Falstaff's remark, "I am not only witty in myself, but the cause that wit is in other men."

Sienkiewicz himself perhaps does not appreciate how much he owes to Shakespeare, or possibly he is a bit sensitive on the subject, for he explains, "If I may be permitted to make a comparison, I think that Zagloba is a better character than Falstaff. At heart the old noble was a good fellow. He would fight bravely when it became necessary, whereas Shakespeare makes Falstaff a coward and a poltroon." [1] If the last two epithets were really an accurate description of Falstaff, he would never have conquered so many millions of readers. [2]

In power of description on a large scale, Sienkiewicz

[1] See Mr. Van Norman's article.

[2] It would be well for Sienkiewicz (and others) to read the brilliant essay that appeared, "by another hand," in the First Series of Mr. Birrell's *Obiter Dicta*.

seems to take a place among the world's great masters of fiction. The bigger the canvas, the more impressive he becomes. His pictures of the boundless steppes by day and night, and in the varying seasons of the year, leave permanent images in the mind. Especially in huge battle scenes is his genius resplendent. It is as if we viewed the whole drama of blood from a convenient mountain peak. The awful tumult gathers and breaks like some hideous storm. So far as I know no writer has ever excelled this Verestchagin of the pen except Tolstoi — and Tolstoi's power lies more in the subjective side of the horrors of war. The Russian's skill is more intellectual, more psychological, of a really higher order of art. For in the endeavour to make the picture vivid, Sienkiewicz becomes at times merely sensational. There is no excuse for his frequent descent into loathsome and horrible detail. The employment of human entrails as a necklace may be historically accurate, but it is out of place in a work of art. The minute description of the use of the stake is another instance of the same tendency, and the unspeakably horrid torture of Azya in *Pan Michael* is a sad blot on an otherwise splendid romance. The love of the physically horrible is an unfortunate characteristic of our Polish novelist, for it appears in *Quo Vadis* as well as in the Trilogy. The greatest works appeal to the mind rather than the senses. *Pan Michael* is a great book, not because it reeks with blood and abounds in hell's ingenuity of pain, but because it presents the character of a hero made perfect through suffering; every sword-stroke develops his spirit as well as his arm. Superfluous events, so frequent in the other works, are here omitted; the story progresses steadily; it is the most condensed and the most human book in the Trilogy. Again, in *The Deluge*, the author's highest skill is shown not in the portrayal of moving accidents by flood and field, but in the regeneration of Kmita. He passes through a long period of slow moral gestation, which ultimately brings him from darkness to light.

To non-Slavonic readers, who became acquainted with Sienkiewicz through the Trilogy, it was a surprise to discover that at home he was equally distinguished as an exponent of modern realism. The acute demand for anything and everything from his pen led to the translation of *The Family of Polanyetski*, rechristened in English (one hardly knows why) *Children of the Soil;* this was preceded by the curious psychological study, *Without Dogma*. It is extremely fortunate that these two works have been made accessible to English readers, for they display powers that would not otherwise be suspected. It is true that English novelists have shone in both realism and romance: we need remember only

Defoe, Dickens, and Thackeray. But at the very moment when we were all thinking of Sienkiewicz as a reincarnation of Scott or Dumas, we were compelled to revise previous estimates of his position and abilities. Genius always refuses to be classified, ticketed, or inventoried; just as you have got your man "placed," or, to change the figure, have solemnly and definitely ushered him to a seat in the second row on the upper tier, you discover that he is much bigger than or quite different from your definition of him. Sienkiewicz is undoubtedly one of the greatest living masters of the realistic novel. In the two stories just mentioned above, the most minute trivialities in human intercourse are set forth in a style that never becomes trivial. He is as good at external description as he is at psychological analysis. He takes all human nature for his province. He belongs not only to the "feel" school of novelists, with Zola, but to the "thought" school, with Turgenev. The workings of the human mind, as impelled by all sorts of motives, ambitions, and passions, make the subject for his examination. In the Trilogy, he took an enormous canvas, and splashed on myriads of figures; in *Without Dogma*, he puts the soul of one man under the microscope. The events in this man's life are mainly "transitions from one state of spiritual experience to another." Naturally the mirror selected is a diary, for *Without*

Dogma belongs to a school of literature illustrated by such examples as the *Sorrows of Werther* and *Amiel's Journal.* It must be remembered that we have here a study primarily of the Slav character. The hero cleverly diagnoses his own symptoms as *Slave Improductivité.* He is perhaps puzzling to the practical Philistine Anglo-Saxon: but not if one has read Turgenev, Dostoievsky, or Gorky. Turgenev's brilliant analysis of Rudin must stand for all time as a perfect portrait of the educated Slav, a person who fulfils the witty definition of a Mugwump, "one who is educated beyond his capacity." We have a similar character here, the conventional conception of Hamlet, a man whose power of reasoning overbalances his strength of will. He can talk brilliantly on all kinds of intellectual topics, but he cannot bring things to pass. He has a bad case of *slave improductivité.* The very title, *Without Dogma,* reveals the lack of conviction that ultimately destroys the hero. He has absolutely no driving power; as he expresses it, *he does not know.* If one wishes to examine this sort of mind, extremely common among the upper classes of Poles and Russians, one cannot do better than read attentively this book. Every futile impulse, every vain longing, every idle day-dream, is clearly reflected. It is a melancholy spectacle, but fascinating and highly instructive. For it is not merely an individual, but the national Slavonic character that is revealed.

Sienkiewicz is not only a Romanticist and a Realist — he is also a Moralist. The foundations of his art are set deep in the bed-rock of moral ideas. As Tolstoi would say, he has the right attitude toward his characters. He believes that the Novel should strengthen life, not undermine it; ennoble, not defile it; for it is good tidings, not evil. " I care not whether the word that I say pleases or not, since I believe that I reflect the great urgent need of the soul of humanity, which is crying for a change. People must think according to the laws of logic. And because they must also live, they want some consolation on the road of life. Masters after the manner of Zola give them only dissolution, chaos, a disgust for life, and despair." [1] This is the signal of a strong and healthy soul. The fact is, that at heart Sienkiewicz is as stout a moralist as Tolstoi, and with equal ardour recognises Christianity as the world's best standard and greatest need. The basis of the novel *Children of the Soil* is purely Christian. The simple-hearted Marynia is married to a man far superior to her in mental endowment and training, as so often happens in Slavonic fiction; she cannot follow his intellectual flights, and does not even understand the processes of his mind.

[1] Taken here and there from his essay on Zola.

She has no talent for metaphysical discussion, and no knowledge of modern science. But although her education does not compare with that of her husband, she has, without suspecting it, completely mastered the art of life; for she is a devout and sincere Christian, meek and lowly in heart. He finally recognises that while he has more learning, she has more wisdom; and when the book closes, we see him a pupil at her feet. All his vain speculations are overthrown by the power of religion manifested in the purity, peace, and contentment of his wife's daily life. And now he too —

> "Leads it companioned by the woman there.
> To live, and see her learn, and learn by her,
> Out of the low obscure and petty world. . . .
> To have to do with nothing but the true,
> The good, the eternal — and these, not alone,
> In the main current of the general life,
> But small experiences of every day,
> Concerns of the particular hearth and home:
> To learn not only by a comet's rush
> But a rose's birth, — not by the grandeur, God —
> But the comfort, Christ."

This idea is revealed positively in *Children of the Soil*, and negatively in *Without Dogma*. The two women, Marynia and Aniela, are very similar. Aniela's intellect is elementary compared with that of her brilliant lover, Leon Ploszowski. But her

Christian faith turns out to be a much better guide to conduct than his flux of metaphysics. She is a good woman, and knows the difference between right and wrong without having to look it up in a book. When he urges her to a *liaison*, and overwhelms her objections with a fine display of modern dialectic, she concludes the debate by saying, "I cannot argue with you, because you are so much cleverer than I; but I know that what you want me to do is wrong, and I will not do it."

We find exactly the same emphasis when we turn to the historical romance *Quo Vadis*. The whole story is a glorification of Christianity, of Christian ethics and Christian belief. The despised Christians have discovered the secret of life, which the culture of Petronius sought in vain. It was hidden from the wise and prudent, and revealed unto babes. The influence of Lygia on Vinicius is, with a totally different environment, precisely the same as the influence of Marynia on Pan Stanislav.

Sienkiewicz seems to have much the same Christian conception of Love as that shown in so many ways by Browning. Love is the *summum bonum*, and every manifestation of it has something divine. Love in all its forms appears in these Polish novels, as it does in Browning, from the basest sensual desire to the purest self-sacrifice. There is indeed a streak of animalism in Sienkiewicz, which shows in all his works; but, if we may believe him, it is merely one representation of the great passion, which so largely controls life and conduct. Love, says Sienkiewicz, with perhaps more force than clearness, should be the foundation of all literature. "L'amour — c'est un droit éternel, une force vitale, c'est le génie — bienfaiteur de notre globe : l'harmonie. Sienkiewicz croit que l'amour, ainsi compris, est le fondement de la littérature polonaise — et que cet amour devrait l'être pour toute la littérature." [1] Some light may be thrown on this statement by a careful reading of *Pan Michael*.

Sienkiewicz is indeed a mighty man — someone has ironically called him a literary blacksmith. There is nothing decadent in his nature. Compared with many English, German, and French writers, who seem at times to express an anæmic and played-out civilisation, he has the very exuberance of power and an endless wealth of material. It is as if the world were fresh and new. And he has not only delighted us with the pageantry of chivalry, and with the depiction of our complex modern civilisation, he has for us also the stimulating influence of a great moral force.

[1] Sent to me by Dr. Glabisz.

VII

HERMANN SUDERMANN

WALKING along Michigan Avenue in Chicago one fine day, I stopped in front of the recently completed hall devoted to music. On the façade of this building had been placed five names, supposed to represent the five greatest composers that the world has thus far seen. It was worth while to pause a moment and to reflect that those five men were all Germans. Germany's contribution to music is not only greater than that of any other nation, it is probably greater than that of all the other countries of the earth put together, and multiplied several times. In many forms of literary art, — especially perhaps in drama and in lyrical poetry, — Germany has been eminent; and she has produced the greatest literary genius since Shakespeare. To-day the Fatherland remains the intellectual workshop of the world; men and women flock thither to study subjects as varied as Theology, Chemistry, Mathematics, and Music. All this splendid achievement in science and in culture makes poverty in the field of prose fiction all the more remarkable. For the fact is, that the total number of truly great world-novels written in the German language, throughout its entire history, can be counted on the fingers of one hand.

In the making of fiction, from the point of view solely of quality, Germany cannot stand an instant's comparison with Russia, whose four great novelists have immensely enriched the world; nor with Great Britain, where masterpieces have been produced for nearly two hundred years; nor with France, where the names of notable novels crowd into the memory; and even America, so poor in literature and in genuine culture, can show at least one romance that stands higher than anything which has come from beyond the Rhine. Germany has no reason to feel ashamed of her barrenness in fiction, so pre-eminent is she in many other and perhaps nobler forms of art. But it is interesting to enquire for a moment into possible causes of this phenomenon, and to see if we can discover why Teutonic fiction is, relatively speaking, so bad.

One dominant fault in most German novels is a lack of true proportion. The principle of selection, which differentiates a painting from a photograph, and makes the artist an Interpreter instead of a Recorder, has been forgotten or overlooked. The high and holy virtue of Omission should be cultivated more sedulously. The art of leaving out is the art that produces the real illusion — where, by the omission of unessential details, things that are salient can be properly emphasised. And what German novels lack is emphasis. This cannot be obtained by merely spacing the letters in descriptions and in conversations; it can be reached only by remembering that prose fiction is as truly an art form as a Sonata. Instead of novels, the weary reader gets long and tiresome biographies of rather unimportant persons; people whom we should not in the least care to know in real life. We follow them dejectedly from the cradle to the grave. Matters of no earthly consequence either to the reader, to the hero, or to the course of the plot, are given as much prominence as great events. In *Jörn Uhl,* to take a recent illustration, the novel is positively choked by trivial detail. Despite the enormous vogue of this story, it does not seem destined to live. It will fall by its own weight.

Another great fault is an excess of sentimentality. For the Germans, who delight in destroying old faiths of humanity, and who remorselessly hammer away at the shrines where we worship in history and religion, are, notwithstanding their iconoclasm, the most sentimental people in the world. Many second- and third-rate German novels are ruined for an Anglo-Saxon reader by a lush streak of sentimental gush, a curious blemish in so intellectual and sceptical a race. This excess of soft material appears in a variety of forms; but to take one common manifestation of it, I should say that the one single object that has done more than anything else to weaken and to destroy German fiction, is the Moon. The Germans are, by nature and by training, scientific; and what their novels need is not the examination of literary critics, but the thoughtful attention of astronomers. The Moon is overworked, and needs a long rest. An immense number of pages are illumined by its chaste beams, for this satellite is both active and ubiquitous. It behaves, it must be confessed, in a dramatic manner, but in a way hopelessly at variance with its methodical and orderly self. In other words, the Moon, in German fiction, is not astronomical, but decorative. I have read some stories where it seems to rise on almost every page, and is invariably full. When Stevenson came to grief on the Moon in *Prince Otto*, he declared that the next time he wrote a novel, he should use an almanac. He unwittingly laid his finger on a weak spot in German fiction. The almanac is, after all, what is most sorely needed. Even Herr Sudermann, for whom we entertain the highest respect, places in *Es War* a young crescent Moon in the eastern sky! But it is in his story, *Der Katzensteg*, that the lunar orb plays its heaviest rôle. It rises so constantly that after a time the very words "*der Mond*" get on one's nerves. At the climax, when the lover looks down on the stream, he there beholds the dead body of his sweetheart. By some scientific process, "unknown to me and which 'twere well to know," she is floating on her back in the water, while the Moon illumines her face, leaving the rest of her remains in darkness. This constitutes a striking picture; and is also of material assistance to the man in locating the whereabouts of the girl. He descends, rescues her from the flood, and digs a grave in which to bury her. The Moon actively and dramatically takes part in this labour. Finally, he has lowered the corpse into the bottom of the cavity. The Moon now shines into the grave in such a manner that the dead woman's face is bright with its rays, whereas the rest of her body and the walls of the tomb are in obscurity. This phenomenon naturally makes a powerful impression on the mourner's mind.

If such things can happen in the works of a writer like Sudermann, one can easily imagine the reckless behaviour of the Moon in the common run of German fiction. The Moon, in fact, is in German novels what the calcium light is in American melodrama. If one "assists " at a performance of, let us say, *No Wedding Bells for Her*, and can take his eye a moment from the stage, he may observe up in the back gallery a person working the calcium light,

and directing its powerful beams in such a fashion
that no matter where the heroine moves, they dwell
exclusively on her face, so that we may contemplate
her features convulsed with emotion. Now in *Der
Katzensteg*, the patient Moon follows the heroine
about with much the same assiduity, and accuracy
of aim. Possibly Herr Sudermann, since the composition of that work, has really consulted an
almanac; for in *Das hohe Lied*, the Moon is practically ignored, and never gets a fair start. Toward the end, I felt sure that it would appear, and
finally, when I came to the words, "The weary disk
of the full moon (*matte Vollmondscheibe*) hung
somewhere in the dark sky," I exclaimed, "Art
thou there, truepenny?" — but the next sentence
showed that the author was playing fast and loose
with his old friend. "It was the illuminated
clock of a railway-station." Can Sudermann have
purposely set a trap for his moon-struck constituency?

From the astronomical point of view, I have seldom
read a novel that contained so much moonlight as
Der Katzensteg, and I have never read one that
contained so little as *Das hohe Lied*. Perhaps
Sudermann is now quietly protesting against what
he himself may regard as a national calamity, for
it is little less than that. Be this as it may, the lack
of proportion and the excess of sentimentality are

two great evils that have militated against the final success of German fiction.

Hermann Sudermann was born at a little village in East Prussia, near the Russian frontier. The natal landscape is dull, depressing, gloomy, and the skies are low and threatening. The clouds return after the rain. Dame Care has spread her grey wings over the flat earth, and neither the scenery nor the quality of the air are such as to inspire hope and vigour. The boy's parents were desperately poor, and the bitter struggles with poverty so frequently described in his novels are reminiscent of early experiences. In the beautiful and affectionate verses, which constitute the dedication to his father and mother, and which are placed at the beginning of *Frau Sorge*, these privations of the Sudermann household are dwelt on with loving tenderness. At the age of fourteen, the child was forced to leave school, and was apprenticed to a chemist — something that recalls chapters in the lives of Keats and of Ibsen. But, like most boys who really long for a good education, Sudermann obtained it; he continued his studies in private, and later returned to school at Tilsit. In 1875 he attended the University at Königsberg, and in 1877 migrated to the University of Berlin. His first impulse was to become a teacher, and he spent several years in a wide range of studies in philosophy and literature. Then he turned to journalism, and edited a political weekly. He finally forsook journalism for literature, and for the last twenty years he has been known in every part of the intellectual world.

Like Mr. J. M. Barrie, Signor D'Annunzio, and other contemporaries, Sudermann has achieved high distinction both as a novelist and as a dramatist. Indeed, one of the signs of the times is the recruiting of playwrights from the ranks of trained experts in prose fiction. It may perhaps be regarded as one more evidence of the approaching supremacy of the Drama, which many literary prophets have foretold. After he had published a small collection of "Zwanglose Geschichten," called *Im Zwielicht*, Sudermann issued his first real novel, *Dame Care* (*Frau Sorge*). This was followed by two tales bound together under the heading *Geschwister*, one of them being the morbidly powerful story, *The Wish* (*Der Wunsch*). Soon after came *Der Katzensteg*, translated into English with the title, *Regina*. Then, after a surprisingly short interval, came his first play, *Die Ehre* (1889), which appeared in the same year as his rival Hauptmann's first drama, *Vor Sonnenaufgang*. *Die Ehre* created a tremendous sensation, and Sudermann was excitedly read and discussed far beyond the limits of his native land. He reached a wild climax of popularity a few years later with his play *Heimat* (English version *Magda*), which has been presented by the greatest actresses in the world, and is familiar to everybody. With the exception of the long novel, *Es War* (English translation, *The Undying Past*), which appeared in 1894, Sudermann devoted himself exclusively to the stage for almost twenty years, and most of us believed he had definitely abandoned novel-writing. From 1889 to 1909, he produced nineteen plays, nearly every one of them successful. Then last year he astonished everybody by publishing a novel of over six hundred closely printed pages, called *Das hohe Lied*, translated into English as *The Song of Songs*. This has had an enormous success, and for 1908–1909, is the best selling work of fiction in the large cities of Germany.

The immense vogue of his early plays had much to do with the wide circulation of his previously published novels. Despite the now universally acknowledged excellence of *Frau Sorge*, it attracted, at the time of its appearance, very little attention. It is going beyond the facts to say with one German critic that "it dropped stillborn from the press"; but it did not give the author anything like the fame he deserved. After the first night of *Die Ehre*, the public became inquisitive. A search was made for everything the new author had written, and the two novels *Frau Sorge*, and the very recent *Katzensteg*, were fairly pounced upon. The small

stock on hand was immediately exhausted, and the
presses poured forth edition after edition. At first
Der Katzensteg received the louder tribute of praise;
it was hailed by many otherwise sane critics as the
greatest work of fiction that Germany had ever
produced. But after the tumult and the shouting
died, the people recognised the superiority of the
former novel. To-day *Der Katzensteg* is, comparatively speaking, little read, and one seldom hears
it mentioned. *Frau Sorge*, on the other hand, has
not only attained more editions than any other work,
either play or novel, by its author, but it bears the
signs that mark a classic. It is one of the very few
truly great German novels, and it is possible that
this early written story will survive everything that
Sudermann has since produced, which is saying a
good deal. It looks like a fixed star.

Sudermann's four novels, *Frau Sorge, Der Katzensteg, Es War,* and *Das hohe Lied,* show a steady
progression in Space as well as in Time. The first
is the shortest; the second is larger; the third is
a long book; the fourth is a leviathan. If novelists
were heard for their much speaking, the order of
merit in this output would need no comment. But
the first of these is almost as superior in quality as
it is inferior in size. When the author prepared
it for the press, he was an absolutely unknown
man. Possibly he put more work on it than went

into the other books, for it apparently bears the marks of careful revision. It is a great exception to the ordinary run of German novels in its complete freedom from superfluous and clogging detail. Turgenev used to write his stories originally at great length, and then reduce them to a small fraction of their original bulk, before offering them to the public. We thus receive the quintessence of his thought and of his art. Now *Frau Sorge* has apparently been subjected to some such process. Much of the huge and varied cargo of ideas, reflections, comments, and speculations carried by the regulation German freight-novel of heavy draught, has here been jettisoned. Then the craft itself has been completely remodelled, and the final result is a thing of grace and beauty.

Frau Sorge is an admirable story in its absolute unity, in its harmonious development, and in its natural conclusion. I do not know of any other German novel that has a more attractive outline. It ought to serve as an example to its author's countrymen.

It is in a way an anatomy of melancholy. It is written throughout in the minor key, and the atmosphere of melancholy envelops it with as much natural charm as though it were a beautiful piece of music. The book is profoundly sad, without any false sentiment and without any revolting coarseness. It is as far removed from the silly sentimentality so common in Teutonic fiction, as it is from the filth of Zola or of Gorky. The deep melancholy of the story is as natural to it as a cloudy sky. The characters live and move and have their being in this grey medium, which fits them like a garment; just as in the early tales of Björnson we feel the strong sunshine and the sharp air. The early environment of the young author, the depressing landscape of his boyhood days, the daily fight with grim want in his father's house — all these elements are faithfully reflected here, and lend their colour to the narrative. And this surrounding melancholy, though it overshadows the whole book, is made to serve an artistic purpose. It contrasts favourably with Ibsen's harsh bitterness, with Gorky's maudlin dreariness, and with the hysterical outbursts of pessimism from the manikins who try to see life from the mighty shoulders of Schopenhauer. At the very heart of the work we find no sentiment of revolt against life, and no cry of despair, but true tenderness and broad sympathy. It is the clear expression of a rich, warm nature.

The story is realistic, with a veil of Romanticism. The various scenes of the tale seem almost photographically real. The daily life on the farm, the struggles with the agricultural machine, the peatbogs, the childish experiences at school, the brutality of the boys, the graphic picture of the funeral, — these would not be out of place in a genuine experimental novel. But we see everything through an imaginative medium, like the impalpable silver-grey mist on the paintings of Andrea del Sarto. The way in which the difficult conception of *Frau Sorge* — part woman, part vague abstraction — is managed, reminds one in its shadowy nature of Nathaniel Hawthorne. This might have been done clumsily, as in a crude fairy-tale, but it exhibits the most subtle art. The first description of Frau Sorge by the mother, the boy's first glimpse of the supernatural woman, his father's overcoat, the Magdalene in church, the flutter of Frau Sorge's wings, — all this gives us a realistic story, and yet takes us into the borderland between the actual and the unknown. From one point of view we have a plain narrative of fact; from another an imaginative poem, and at the end we feel that both have been marvellously blended.

The simplicity of the style gives the novel a high rank in German prose. It has that naïve quality wherein the Germans so greatly excel writers in other languages. It is a surprising fact that this tongue, so full of difficulties for foreigners, and which seems often so confused and involved, can, in the hands of a master, be made to speak like a little child. The literary style of *Frau Sorge* is

naïve without ever being trivial or absurd. It is
pleasant to observe, by the way, that to some extent
this book is filling the place in American educational
programmes of German that *L'Abbé Constantin*
has for so long a time occupied in early studies of
French. Both novels are masterpieces of simplicity.

But what we remember the most vividly, years
after we have finished this story, is not its scenic
background, nor its unearthly charm, nor the grace
of its style; it is the character and temperament of
the boy-hero. It is the first, and possibly the best,
of Sudermann's remarkable psychological studies.
The whole interest is centred in young Paul. He is
not exactly the normal type of growing boy, — compare him with Tom Sawyer ! — but because he is not
ordinary, it does not follow that he is unnatural.
To many thoroughly respectable Philistine readers,
he may appear not only abnormal, but impossible;
but the book was not intended for Philistines. I
believe that this boy is absolutely true to life, though
I do not recall at this moment any other novel where
this particular kind of youth occupies the centre of
the stage.

For *Frau Sorge* is a careful study and analysis
of *bashfulness*, a characteristic that causes more
exquisite torture to many boys and girls than is
commonly recognised. Many of us, when we laugh
at a boy's bashfulness, are brutal, when we mean to

be merely jocular. Paul is intensely self-conscious. He is not at all like a healthy, practical, objective child, brought up in a large family, and surrounded by the noisy progeny of neighbours. His life is perforcedly largely subjective. He would give anything could he associate with schoolmates with the ease that makes a popular boy sure of his welcome. His accursed timidity makes him invariably show his most awkward and unattractive side. He is not in the least a *Weltkind*. He has none of the coarseness and none of the clever shirking of work and study so characteristic of the perfectly normal small boy. He does his duty *without any reservations*, and without understanding why. The narrative of his mental life is deeply pathetic. It is impossible to read the book without a lump in the throat.

Paul is finally saved from himself by the redeeming power of love. The little heroine Elsbeth is shadowy, — a merely conventional picture of hair, complexion, and eyes, — but she is, after all, *das Ewigweibliche*, and draws Paul upward and onward. She rescues him from the Slough of Despond. There is no touch of cynicism here. Sudermann shows us the healing power of a good woman's heart.

The next novel, *Der Katzensteg*, is more pretentious than *Frau Sorge*, but not nearly so fine a book. It abounds in dramatic scenes, and glows with fierce passion. It seems more like a melodrama than a story, and it is not surprising that its author immediately discovered — perhaps in the very composition of this romance — his genius for the stage. It is a historical novel, but the chief interest, as always in Sudermann, is psychological. The element of Contrast — so essential to true drama, and which is so strikingly employed in *Die Ehre*, *Sodoms Ende*, *Heimat*, and *Johannes* — is the mainspring of *Der Katzensteg*. We have here the irrepressible conflict between the artificial and the natural. The heroine of the story is a veritable child of nature, with absolutely elemental passions, as completely removed from civilisation as a wild beast. She was formerly the mistress of the hero's father, and for a long time is naturally regarded with loathing by the son. But she transfers her dog-like fidelity from the dead parent to the morbid scion of the house. The more cruelly the young man treats her, the deeper becomes her love for him. Nor does he at first suspect the hold she has on his heart. He imagines himself to be in love with the pastor's daughter in the village, who has been brought up like a hothouse plant. This simpering, affected girl, who has had all the advantages of careful nurture and education, is throughout the story contrasted with the wild flower, Regina. The contrast is thorough — mental, moral, physical. The educated girl has no real mind; she has only accomplishments. Her morality has nothing to do with the heart; it is a bundle of conventions. And finally, while Regina has a magnificent, voluptuous physique, the hero discovers — by the light of the moon — that the lady of his dreams is too thin! This is unendurable. He rushes away from the town to the heights where stands his lonely dwelling, cursing himself for his folly in being so long blind to the wonderful charm and devotion of the passionate girl who, he feels sure, is waiting for him. He hastens on the very wings of love, wild with his new-found happiness. But the very fidelity of the child of nature has caused her death. She stood out on the bridge — *der Katzensteg* — to warn her lover of his danger. There she is shot by her drunken father, and the impatient lover sees her dead body in the stream below.

Now he has leisure to reflect on what a fool he has been. He sees how much nobler are natural passions than artificial conventions. Regina had lived "on the other side of good and evil," knowing and caring nothing for the standards of society. The entire significance of the novel is summed up in this paragraph: —

"And as he thought and pondered, it seemed to him as if the clouds which separate the foundations of human being from human consciousness" (that is, things as they are from our conceptions of them, — *den Boden des menschlichen Seins vom menschlichen Bewusstsein*) "were dispersed, and he saw a space deeper than men commonly see, into the depths of the unconscious. That which men call Good and Bad, moved restless in the clouds around the surface; below, in dreaming strength, lay the *Natural* (*das Natürliche*). 'Whom Nature has blessed,' he said to himself, 'him she lets safely grow in her dark depths and allows him to struggle boldly toward the light, without the clouds of Wisdom and Error surrounding and bewildering him.'"

But there is nothing new or original in this doctrine, however daring it may be. One can find it all in Nietzsche and in Rousseau. The best thing about the novel is that it once more illustrates Sudermann's sympathy for the outcast and the despised.

An extraordinarily powerful study in morbid psychology is shown in one of his short stories, called *Der Wunsch*. The tale is told backward. It begins with the discovery of a horrible suicide, the explanation of which is furnished to the prostrated lover by the dead woman's manuscript. A man and his wife, at first happily married, encounter the dreadful obstacles of poverty and disease; the fatal illness of his wife plunges the husband into a hard, bitter melancholy. From this he is partially saved by the appearance of his wife's younger sister on the scene, who comes to take care of the sick woman. The close companionship of the two, previously fond of each other, and now united daily by their care of the invalid, results in love; but both are absolutely loyal to the suffering wife. They cannot help thinking, however, of the wonderful happiness that might be theirs, were the man free; nevertheless, they do everything possible to solace the last hours of the woman for whom they feel an immense compassion. One night, as the sister watches at the bedside, and gazes on the face of her sister, she suddenly feels the uncontrollable and fatal *wish* — "Would that she might die!" She is so smitten with remorse that after the death of the invalid she commits suicide. For although her wish had nothing to do with this event, she nevertheless regards herself as a murderer, and goes to self-execution. The physician remarks that this psychological *wish* is not uncommon; that during his professional services he has often seen it legibly written on the faces of relatives by the bedside — sometimes actuated by avarice, sometimes by other forms of personal greed.

The next regular novel, *Es War*, is the study of a past sin on a man's character, temperament, and conduct. The hero, Leo, has committed adultery with the wife of a disagreeable husband, and, being challenged by the latter to a duel, has killed him. Thus having broken two of the commandments, he departs for South America, where for four years he lives a joyous, care-free, savage existence, with murder and sensuality a regular part of the day's work. It is perhaps a little hard on South America that Leo could live there in such liberty and return to Germany unscathed by the arm of the law; but this is essential to the story. He returns a kind of Superman, rejoicing in his magnificent health and absolutely determined to repent nothing. He will not allow the past to obscure his happiness. But unfortunately his friend Ulrich, whom he has loved since childhood with an affection passing the love of women, has married the guilty widow, in blissful unconsciousness of his friend's guilt. And here the story opens. It is a long, depressing, but intensely interesting tale. At the very close, when it seems that wholesale tragedy is inevitable, the clouds lift, and Leo, who has found the Past stronger than he, regains something of the cheerfulness that characterises his first appearance in the narrative. Nevertheless *es war;* the Past cannot be lightly tossed aside or forgotten. It comes near wrecking the lives of every important character in the novel. Yet the idea at the end seems to be that although sin entails fearful punishment, and the scars can never be obliterated, it is possible to triumph over it and find happiness once more. The most beautiful and impressive thing in *Es War* is the friendship between the two men — so different in temperament and so passionately devoted to each other. A large group of characters is splendidly kept in hand, and each is individual and clearly drawn. One can never forget the gluttonous, wine-bibbing Parson, who comes eating and drinking, but who is a terror to publicans and sinners.

Last year appeared *Das hohe Lied*, which, although it lacks the morbid horror of much of Sudermann's work, is the most pessimistic book he has ever written. The irony of the title is the motive of the whole novel. Between the covers of this thick volume we find the entire detailed life-history of a woman. She passes through much debauchery, and we follow her into many places where we should hesitate to penetrate in real life. But the steps in her degradation are not put in, as they so often are in Guy de Maupassant, merely to lend spice to the narrative; every event has a definite influence on the heroine's character. The story, although very long, is strikingly similar to that in a recent successful American play, *The Easiest Way*. Lilly Czepanek is not naturally base or depraved. The manuscript roll of her father's musical composition, *Das hohe Lied*, which she carries with her from childhood until her final submission to circumstances, and which saves her body from suicide but not her soul from death, is emblematic of the *élan* which she has in her heart. With the best intentions in the world, with noble, romantic sentiments, with a passionate desire to be a rescuing angel to

the men and women whom she meets, she gradually
sinks in the mire, until, at the end, her case is hopeless. She struggles desperately, but each struggle
finds her stock of resistance reduced. She always
ends by taking the easiest way. Like a person in
a quicksand, every effort to escape sinks the body
deeper; or, like a drowning man, the more he raises
his hands to heaven, the more speedy is his destruction.
Much of Lilly's degradation is caused by what she
believes to be an elevating altruistic impulse. And
when she finally meets the only man in her whole
career who respects her in his heart, who really
means well by her, and whose salvation she can
accomplish along with her own, — one single evening, where she begins with the best of intentions
and with a sincere effort toward a higher plane,
results in complete damnation. Then, like the
heroine in *The Easiest Way*, she determines to commit suicide, and really means to do it. But the same
weakness that has made it hitherto impossible for
her to triumph over serious obstacles, prevents her
from taking this last decisive step. As she hears
the splash of her talisman in the cold, dark water,
she realises that she is not the stuff of which heroine
are made, either in life or in death.

"And as she heard that sound, then she knew instantly
that she would *never* do it. — No indeed! Lilly Czepanek
was *no* Heroine. *No* martyr of her love was Lilly Czepanek.

No Isolde, who in the determination not to be, sees the highest self-assertion. She was only a poor brittle, crushed, broken thing, who must drag along through her days as best she can."

And with this realisation she goes wearily back to a rich lover she had definitely forsaken, knowing that in saving her life she has now lost it for ever.

This is the last page of the story, but unfortunately it does not end here. Herr Sudermann has chosen to add one paragraph after the word " *Schluss*." By this we learn that in the spring of the following year the aforesaid rich lover *marries* Lilly, and takes her on a bridal trip to Italy, which all her life had been in her dreams the celestial country. She is thus saved from the awful fate of the streets, which during the whole book had loomed threatening in the distance. But this ending leaves us completely bewildered and depressed. It seems to imply that, after all, these successive steps in moral decline do not make much difference, one way or the other; for at the very beginning of her career she could not possibly have hoped for any better material fate than this. The reader not only feels cheated; he feels that the moral element in the story, which through all the scenes of vice has been made clear, is now laughed at by the author. This is why I call the book the most pessimistic of all Sudermann's writings. A novel may take us through woe and sin, and yet not produce any impression of cyni-

cism; but one that makes a careful, serious study
of subtle moral decay through over six hundred
pages, and then implies at the end that the distinction between vice and virtue is, after all, a matter
of no consequence, leaves an impression for which
the proverbial "bad taste in the mouth" is utterly
inadequate to describe. Some years ago, Professor
Heller, in an admirable book on Modern German
Literature, remarked, in a comparison between
Hauptmann and Sudermann, that the former has
no working theory of life, which the latter possessed.
That Hauptmann's dramas offer no solution, merely
giving sordid wretchedness; while Sudermann shows
the conquest of environment by character. Or, as
Mr. Heller puts it, there is the contrast between
the "driving and the drifting." I think this distinction in the main will justify itself to anyone who
makes a thoughtful comparison of the work of these
two remarkable men. Despite the depreciation
of Sudermann and the idolatry of Hauptmann, an
attitude so fashionable among German critics at
present, I believe that the works of the former have
shown a stronger grasp of life. But the final paragraph of *Das hohe Lied* is a staggering blow to
those of us who have felt that Sudermann had some
kind of a *Weltanschauung*. It is like Chopin's
final movement in his great Sonata; mocking laughter follows the solemn tones of the Funeral March.

Up to this last bad business, *Das hohe Lied* exhibits that extraordinary power of psychological analysis that we have come to expect from Sudermann. Lilly, apart from her personal beauty, is not, after all, an interesting girl; her mind is thoroughly shallow and commonplace. Nor are the numerous adventures through which she passes particularly interesting. And yet the long book is by no means dull, and one reads it with steady attention. The reason for this becomes clear, after some reflexion. Not only are we absorbed by the contemplation of so masterly a piece of mental analysis, but what interests us most is the constant attempt of Lilly to analyse herself. We often wonder how people appear to themselves. The unspoken dialogues between Lilly and her own soul are amazingly well done. She is constantly surprised by herself, constantly bewildered by the fact that what she thought was one set of motives, turns out to be quite otherwise. All this comes to a great climax in the scene late at night when she writes first one letter, then another — each one meaning to be genuinely confessional. Each letter is to give an absolutely faithful account of her life, with a perfectly truthful depiction of her real character. Now the two letters are so different that in one she appears to be a low-lived adventuress, and in the other a noble woman, deceived through what is noblest in her. Finally

she tears both up, for she realises that although
each letter gives the facts, neither tells the truth.
And then she sees that the truth cannot be told;
that life is far too complex to be put into language.

In the attempts of German critics years ago to
"classify" Sudermann, he was commonly placed
in one of the three following groups. Many insisted that he was merely a Decadent, whose pleasure
it was to deal in unhealthy social problems. That
his interest in humanity was pathological. Others
held that he was a fierce social Reformer, a kind of
John the Baptist, who wished to reconstruct modern
society along better lines, and who was therefore
determined to make society realise its own rotten-
ness. He was primarily a Satirist, not a Decadent.
Professor Calvin Thomas quoted (without appro-
bation) Professor Litzmann of Bonn, who said that
Sudermann was "a born satirist, not one of the tame
sort who only tickle and scratch, but one of the
stamp of Juvenal, who swings his scourge with fierce
satisfaction so that the blood starts from the soft,
voluptuous flesh." A reading of *Das hohe Lied*
will convince anyone that Sudermann, wherever
he is, is not among the prophets. Finally, there
were many critics who at the very start recognised
Sudermann as primarily an artist, who chooses to
paint the aspects of life that interest him. This
is undoubtedly the true viewpoint. We may regret

that he prefers to analyse human characters in morbid and abnormal development, but that, after all, is his affair, and we do not have to read him unless we wish to. Professor Thomas, in an admirable article on *Das Glück im Winkel*, contributed in 1895 to the New York *Nation*, said, "Sudermann is a man of the world, a psychologist, and an artist, not a voice crying in the wilderness. The immortality of Juvenal or Jeremiah would not be to his taste." It is vain to quarrel with the direction taken by genius, however much we may deplore its course. Sudermann is one of the greatest, if not the greatest, of Germany's living writers, and every play or novel from his pen contains much material for serious thought.

VIII

ALFRED OLLIVANT

In the month of September, 1898, there appeared
in America a novel with the attractive title, *Bob,
Son of Battle*. Unheralded by author's fame or by
the blare of advertisement, it was at first unnoticed;
but in about a twelvemonth everybody was talking
about it. It became one of the "best sellers";
unlike its companions, it has not vanished with
the snows of yesteryear. At this moment it is being
read and reread all over the United States. I do
not believe there is a single large town in our country
where the book is unknown, or where a reference
to it fails to bring to the faces of intelligent people
that glow of reminiscent delight aroused by the
memory of happy hours passed in the world of imagination. It seemed so immensely superior to the
ordinary run of new novels, that we gazed with
pardonable curiosity at the unfamiliar signature on
the title-page. Who was this writer who knew so
much of the nature of dogs and men? Where had
he found that extraordinarily vivid style, and what

experiences had he passed through that gave him his subtle insight into character? But all that we could then discover was that Alfred Ollivant was an Englishman, and that *Bob* was his first novel. We decided that he must have lived long, observed all kinds of dogs, and a large variety of men, women, and children; and that for some reason best known to himself he had chosen to print nothing until he had descended into the vale of years. For only the other day we were not surprised to find that *Joseph Vance* was the winter fruit of a man nearly seventy; that book at any rate was the expression of a man who had had life, and had it abundantly.

Our astonishment was keen indeed when we learned that the author of *Bob* was a boy just out of his teens, who had written his wonderful book in horizontal pain and weakness. He had entered the army, receiving his commission as a cavalry officer in 1893, at the age of nineteen; a few weeks after this event, a fall from his horse injured his spine, previously affected by some mysterious malady; this accident abruptly checked his chosen military career, and made him a man of letters. Literature owes a great deal to enforced idleness, whether the writer be sick or in prison. The wind bloweth where it listeth; and we perceived once more that genius does not always accompany good health, or maturity, or ambition; it seems to select with absolute caprice the individuals through whom it speaks. And so this first-born child of the brain was delivered, like human infants, on a bed of suffering; being, to complete the analogy, none the less healthy on that account. The book was begun in 1894, when the author was twenty years old; during intervals of physical capacity in 1895 and 1896, it was continued, and was submitted to the publishers in 1897.

It was to have been published in the autumn, but the London firm decided to postpone its appearance one year. The author employed these months in completely rewriting the story, which he had named *Owd Bob*. Meanwhile, the New York publishers, who had a copy of the original manuscript, fearing that the title *Owd Bob* lacked magnetism, wisely rechristened it *Bob, Son of Battle*. And so, in September, 1898, the novel in its first form, but with a new name, was printed in America; simultaneously in England it appeared in a new form, but with the old name. In other words, the London first edition, *Owd Bob*, is a thoroughly revised version of the American first edition, *Bob, Son of Battle*, although they were published at the same time. It does not seem as though the author could have improved a book that so completely satisfies us as it stands; and Americans, to whom *Owd Bob* is unknown, may not be-

lieve that it can be superior to *Bob, Son of Battle.*
Nevertheless it is. The two versions are of course
alike in general features of the plot and in outline;
but no one who has read both can hesitate an instant.
One has only to compare the manner in which Red
Wull made his *début* in America with the chapter
where he first appears (in a totally different way)
in the English edition, to see how clearly second
thoughts were best.

And yet, despite the enormous popularity of *Bob,
Son of Battle* in the United States, and despite the
fact that Englishmen had the opportunity to read
the story in a still finer form, it has not until very
recently made any impression on British readers
or on London critics. Is it possible that a book,
like a dog, may be killed by a bad name? The
novel was written by an Englishman, the scenes were
laid in Britain, it dealt with manners and customs
peculiarly English, and it was aimed directly at
an English public. And yet, for nearly ten years
after its publication, *Owd Bob* remained in obscurity.[1]
But its day is coming, and the prophet will yet receive honour in his own country. In 1908 it was
reprinted in a seven-pence edition, of which fifty

[1] A year or two ago I asked one of the foremost English dramatists, one of the foremost English novelists, and one of the
foremost English critics, men whose names are known everywhere
in America, if they had read *Bob;* not one of them had ever heard
of the book.

thousand copies have already seen the light. This is nothing to the American circulation; but it is promising. Bearing in mind the futility of literary prophecy, I still believe that the day will come when *Owd Bob* will be generally recognised as belonging to English literature.

The splendid fidelity and devotion of the dog to his master have certainly been in part repaid by men of letters in all stages of the world's history. A valuable essay might be written on the dog's contributions to literature; in the poetry of the East, hundreds of years before Christ, the poor Indian insisted that his four-footed friend should accompany him into eternity. We know that this bit of Oriental pathos impressed Pope: —

> "But thinks, admitted to that equal sky,
> His faithful dog shall bear him company."

One of the most profoundly affecting incidents in the *Odyssey* is the recognition of the ragged Ulysses by the noble old dog, who dies of joy. During the last half-century, since the publication of Dr. John Brown's *Rab and his Friends* (1858), the dog has approached an apotheosis. Among innumerable sketches and stories with canine heroes may be mentioned Bret Harte's brilliant portrait of *Boonder;* Maeterlinck's essay on dogs; Richard Harding Davis's *The Bar Sinister;* Stevenson's whimsical comments on *The Character of Dogs;* Kipling's *Garm;* and Jack London's initial success, *The Call of the Wild*.[1] But all these latter-day pamphlets, good as they are, fail to reach the excellence of *Bob, Son of Battle*. It is the best dog story ever written, and it inspires regret that dogs cannot read.

No one who knows Mr. Ollivant's tale can by any possibility forget the Grey Dog of Kenmuir — the perfect, gentle knight — or the thrilling excitement of his successful struggles for the cup. He is indeed a noble and beautiful character, with the Christian combination of serpent and dove. But Owd Bob in a slight degree shares the fate of all beings who approach moral perfection. He reminds us at times of Tennyson's Arthur in the *Idylls of the King*, though he fortunately delivers no lectures. Lancelot was wicked, and Arthur was good; but Lancelot has the touch of earth that makes him interesting, and Arthur has more than a touch of boredom. In *Paradise Lost* the spotless Raphael does not compare in charm with the picturesque Foe of God and Man. The real hero in Milton, as I suspect the poet very well knew, is the Devil; and if Mr. Ollivant had ignored both English and

[1] One may fairly class with this literature the remarkable speech on dogs delivered in his youth in a courtroom by the late Senator Vest. The speech won the case against the evidence.

American godfathers, and called his novel *The Tailless Tyke*, no reader could have objected. Red Wull is the Satan of this canine epic; he has for us a fascination at once horrible and irresistible. The author seems to have felt that the Grey Dog was overshadowed; and he has saved our active sympathy for him by the clever device of making him at one time dangerously ill, when we realise how much we love him; and finally by throwing him under awful suspicion, that we may experience — as we certainly do — the enormous relief of beholding him guiltless. But in spite of our best instincts, Red Wull is the protagonist. Dog and master have never been matched in a more sinister manner than Adam McAdam and the Tailless Tyke. Bill Sikes and his companion are nothing to it, and we cannot help remembering that to the eternal disgrace of dogs, Bill Sikes's last friend forsook him. Compared with Red Wull, the Hound of the Baskervilles is a pet lapdog. When Adam and Wullie appear upon the scene, we look alive, even as their virtuous enemies were forced to do, for we know something is bound to happen. When the little man is greeted with a concert of hoots and jeers, we cannot repress some sympathy for him, akin to our feeling toward the would-be murderer Shylock, silent and solitary under the noisy taunts of the feather-headed Gratiano. This bitter and lonely wretch is a real character, and his strange personality is presented with extraordinary skill. There is not a single false touch from first to last; and the little man with the big dog abides in our memory. Red Wull is the hero of a hundred fights; his tremendous and terrible exploits are the very essence of piratical romance. After he has slain the two huge beasts of the showman, McAdam exclaims with a sob of paternal pride, "Ye play so rough, Wullie!"

And the death of the Tailless Tyke is positively Homeric. The other dogs, all his ruthless enemies, whisper to each other and silently steal from the room. They know that the hour has struck, and that this will be the last fight. The whole pack set upon him, each one goaded by the remembrance of some murdered relative, or by some humiliating scar. Red Wull asks nothing better than meeting them all; and the unequal combat becomes a frightful carnage. At the very end, as much exhausted by the labour of killing as by his own wounds, the great dog — now red indeed — hears his master's familiar cry, "Wullie, to me!" and with a super-canine effort he raises his dying form from the bottom of the writhing mass, shakes off the surviving foes, and slowly staggers to McAdam's feet. Like Samson, the dead which he slew at his death were more than they which he slew in his life.

Mr. Ollivant's next book, *Danny*, also a dog story, was not nearly so effective. The human characters command the most attention, though the old man with the weeping eye becomes a bit wearisome. The passages of pure nature description are often exquisitely written, and prove that at heart the author is a poet. But in the narrative portions there is an unfortunate attempt to conceal the slightness of the story by preciosity and affectation in the style. For the simple truth is that in *Danny* there is no story worth the telling. We recall distinctly the lovely young wife and her grim ironclad of a husband, but just what happened between the covers of the book escapes us. Although Mr. Ollivant believes in *Danny*, in spite of or because of its lack of popularity, he was so dissatisfied with the American edition that he suppressed it. Such an act is an indication of the high artistic standard that he has set for himself; ambitious as he is, he would rather merit fame than have it.

While the readers of *Bob* and of *Danny* were guessing what kind of a dog the young author would select for his next novel, he surprised us all by writing an uncaninical work. This story, adorned with happy illustrations, and printed in big type, as though for the eyes of children, was called *Red-Coat Captain*, and was enigmatically located in

"That Country." Every American publisher to
whom the manuscript was offered, rejected it, saying emphatically that it was nonsense; and if there
had not been a strain of idealism in the Head of
the firm that reconsidered and finally printed it,
the book would probably never have felt the press.
Mr. Ollivant was sure that the story would appeal
at first only to a very few, and he requested the
publisher not only to refrain from issuing any advertisement, but to make the entire first edition
consist of only three copies — one for the archives of
the House, one for the author, and one for a believing friend. The children of this world are wiser
in their generation than the children of light; and
the shrewd man of business did not take the peti-
tion very seriously. The verdict Nonsense has been
loudly ratified by many reviewers and readers; to
the few it has been wisdom, to the many foolish-
ness. For, as was said years ago of a certain
poem, "The capacity to understand such a work
must be spiritual." It matters not how clever one
may be, how well read, how sensitive to artistic
beauties and defects; qualities of a totally different
nature must be present, and even then the time and
place must be right, if one is to seize the inner meaning of *Red-Coat Captain*. I was about to say, the
inner meaning of a story *like Red-Coat Captain*,
but I was stopped by the thought that no story like

it has ever been published, and perhaps never will be. Both conception and expression are profoundly original, and, in spite of some failure of articulation, the work is strongly marked with genius. It is an allegory based on the eleventh and twelfth commandments, which we have good authority for believing are worth all the ten put together. From one point of view it is a book for children; the mysterious setting of the tale is sure to appeal to certain imaginative boys and girls. But the early chapters, dealing with the pretty courtship and the honeymoon, will be fully appreciated only by those who have some years to their credit or otherwise. There is in this story the ineffable charm and fragrance of purity. It is the lily in its author's garden.

Mr. Ollivant's latest novel is the most conventional of the four, and wholly unlike any of its predecessors. It is a rattling, riotous romance, placed in the troublous times of the Napoleonic wars. The mighty shadow of Nelson falls darkly across the narrative, but the author has not committed the sin — so common in historical romances — of making a historical character the chief of the *dramatis personæ*. The title rôle is played by *The Gentleman*, and he is a hero worthy of Cooper or of Stevenson. Marked by reckless audacity, brilliant in swordplay and in horsemanship, clever in turn of speech, gifted with the manner of a pre-Revolu-

tion Duke — what more in the heroic line can a
reader desire? The architecture of the novel and
the staccato paragraphs infallibly remind one of
Victor Hugo, whom, however, Mr. Ollivant does
not know. Nor, outside of the works of Stevenson,
have we ever seen a story minus love so steadily
interesting. It is an amphibious book, and those
who like fighting on land and sea may have their fill.
The percentage of mortality is high; soldiers and
sailors die numerously, and the hideous details of
death are worthy of *La Débâcle;* there is a welter
of gore. If this were all that could be said, if the
fascination of this romance depended wholly on
the crowded action, it would simply be one more
exciting tale added to the hundreds published every
year; good to read on train and turbine, but not
worth serious attention or criticism. But the incidents, while frequent and thrilling, are not, at
least to the discriminating reader, the main thing,
as the Germans say. Nor is the construction, clever
enough, nor the characters, real as they are; the
main thing is the style, which, quite different from
that in his former books, is yet all his own. The
style, in the best sense of the word, is pictorial; it
transforms the past into the present. The succession of events rolls off like a glowing panorama.
It is perhaps natural that many reviewers should
have praised *The Gentleman* more highly than all

the rest of Mr. Ollivant's work put together; but, notwithstanding its wider appeal, it lacks the permanent qualities of *Bob*, and (I believe) of *Red-Coat Captain*, for they are original.

That Mr. Ollivant is now on the road to physical health will be good news. He has already done work that no one else can do, and we cannot spare him. His four novels indicate versatility as well as much greater gifts; and he should be watched by all who take an interest in contemporary literature and who believe that the future is as rich as the past. *Bob* looks like the best English novel that has appeared between *Tess of the D'Urbervilles* in 1891, and *Joseph Vance* in 1906. Nothing but bodily obstacles can prevent its author from going far.

IX

ROBERT LOUIS STEVENSON

STEVENSON spent his life, like an only and lonely child, in playing games with himself. Most boys who read romances have the dramatic instinct; they must forthwith incarnate the memories of their reading, and anything will do for a *mise en scène*. The mudpuddle becomes an ocean, where the pirate ship is launched; a scrubby apple tree has infinite possibilities. Armed with a wooden sword, the child sallies forth in the rain, and fiercely cuts down the mulleins; could we only see him without being seen, we should observe the wild light in his eye, and the frown of battle on his brow. He walks cautiously in the underbrush, to surprise the ambushed foe; and it is with rapture that he goes to sleep in a tent, pitched six yards from the kitchen door. This spirit of adventure remains in some men's hearts, even after the hair has grown grey or gone; they hear the call of the wild, lock up the desk, go into the woods, and there rejoice in a process of decivilisation.

In order to enjoy life, one must love it; and nobody ever loved life more than Stevenson. "It is better to be a fool than to be dead," said he. To him the world was always picturesque, whether he saw it through the mists of Edinburgh, or amid the snows of Davos, or in the tropical heat of Samoa. "Where is Samoa?" asked a friend. "Go out of the Golden Gate," replied Stevenson, "and take the first turn to the left." This counsel makes up in joyous imagination what it lacks in latitude and longitude. Everything in Stevenson's bodily and mental life was an adventure, to be begun in a spirit of reckless enthusiasm. In his travels with a donkey, he was a beloved vagabond, whose wayside acquaintances are to be envied; in compulsory expeditions in search of health, he set out with as much zest as though he were after buried treasure; everything was an adventure, and his marriage was the greatest adventure of all. He read books with the same enthusiasm with which he tramped, or paddled in a canoe; every new novel he opened with the spirit of an explorer, for who knows in its pages what people one may meet? William Archer sent him a copy of Bernard Shaw's story, *Cashel Byron's Profession*, and Stevenson wrote in reply from Saranac Lake, "Over Bashville the footman I howled with derision and delight; I dote on Bashville — I could read of him for ever; *de Bashville je suis le fervent* — there is only one Bashville, and I am his devoted slave. . . . It is all mad, mad and deliriously delightful. . . . It is HORRID FUN. . . . (I say, Archer, my God, what women !)" What would authors give for a reading public like that?

Prone in bed, when his attention was not diverted by a hemorrhage, he lived amid the pageantry of gorgeous day-dreams, presented on the stage of his brain. We know that Ben Jonson saw the Romans and Carthaginians fighting, marching and countermarching, across his great toe. Stevenson would have understood this perfectly. No pain or sickness ever daunted him, or held him captive; his mind was always in some picturesque or immensely interesting place. In composition, he seemed to have a double consciousness; he moulded his sentences with the fastidious care of a great artist; at the same moment he felt the growing sea-breeze, and knew that his hero would very soon have to shorten sail.

It is pleasant to remember that a man who had such genius for friendship, who so generously admired the literary work of his contemporaries, and who loved the whole world of saints and sinners, received such widespread homage in return. His career as a man of letters extended over twenty years; and during the last eight his name was actually a household word. To be sure, he published much work of a high order without getting even a hearing; his *Inland Voyage, Travels with a Donkey, Virginibus Puerisque, Familiar Studies, New Arabian Nights*, and even *Treasure Island*, attracted very little attention; he remained in obscurity. But when, in the year 1886, appeared the *Strange Case of Dr. Jekyll and Mr. Hyde*, he found himself famous; the thrilling excitement of the story, combined with its powerful moral appeal, simply conquered the world. And although his own plays were failures, he had the satisfaction of knowing that thousands of people in theatres were spellbound by the modern Morality made out of his novel. Few writers have become "classics" in so short a time; during the years that remained to him, he was compelled to prepare a superb edition of his *Complete Works*. Without ever appealing to the animal nature of humanity, he had the keen satisfaction of reigning in the hearts of uncultivated readers, and of receiving the almost universal tribute of refined critics. There are authors who are the delight of a bookish few, and there are authors with an enormous public and no reputation. There are poets like Donne, and prose-masters like Browne, precious to the men and women of patrician taste; and there are some familiar examples of the other kind, needless to call by name. Stevenson pleases us all; for he always has a good story, and the subtlety of his art gives to his narrative imperishable beauty.

Stevenson's appearance as a novelist was in itself
an adventure. He seemed at first as obsolete as
a soldier of fortune. He was as unexpected and
as picturesque among contemporary writers of fiction
as an Elizabethan knight in a modern drawing-
room. When he placed *Treasure Island* on the
literary map, Realism was at its height in some
localities, and at its depth in others. But it was
everywhere the standard form, in which young
writers strove to embody their visions. Zola had
just made an address in which he remarked that
Walter Scott was dead, and that the fashion of his
style had passed away. The experimental novel
would go hand in hand with the advance of scientific
thought. And there were many who believed that
Zola spoke the truth. This state of affairs was a
tremendous challenge to Stevenson, and he accepted
it in the spirit of chivalry. The very name of his
first novel, *Treasure Island*, was like the flying of
a flag. Those critics who saw it must have smiled,
and shaken their wise heads, for had not the time
for such follies gone by? Stevenson was fully aware
of what he was doing; in the midst of contemporary
fiction he felt as impatient and as ill at ease as a
boy, imprisoned in a circle of elders, whose conversation does not in the least interest him. His
sentiments are clearly shown in a letter to the late
Mr. Henley, written shortly after the appearance of

Treasure Island, and which is important enough to quote somewhat fully: —

"I do desire a book of adventure — a romance — and no man will get or write me one. Dumas I have read and reread too often; Scott, too, and I am short. I want to hear swords clash. I want a book to begin in a good way; a book, I guess, like *Treasure Island,* alas! which I have never read, and cannot though I live to ninety. I would God that someone else had written it! By all that I can learn, it is the very book for my complaint. I like the way I hear it opens; and they tell me John Silver is good fun. And to me it is, and must ever be, a dream unrealised, a book unwritten. O my sighings after romance, or even Skeltery, and O! the weary age which will produce me neither!

CHAPTER I

The night was damp and cloudy, the ways foul. The single horseman, cloaked and booted, who pursued his way across Willesden Common, had not met a traveller, when the sound of wheels —

CHAPTER I

'Yes, sir,' said the old pilot, 'she must have dropped into the bay a little afore dawn. A queer craft she looks.'

'She shows no colours,' returned the young gentleman, musingly.

'They're a-lowering of a quarter-boat, Mr. Mark,' resumed the old salt. 'We shall soon know more of her.'

'Ay,' replied the young gentleman called Mark, 'and here, Mr. Seadrift, comes your sweet daughter Nancy tripping down the cliff.'

'God bless her kind heart, sir,' ejaculated old Seadrift.

CHAPTER I

The notary, Jean Rossignol, had been summoned to the top of a great house in the Isle St. Louis to make a will; and now, his duties finished, wrapped in a warm roquelaure and with a lantern swinging from one hand, he issued from the mansion on his homeward way. Little did he think what strange adventures were to befall him! —

That is how stories should begin. And I am offered HUSKS instead.

What should be:	What is:
The Filibuster's Cache.	Aunt Anne's Tea Cosy.
Jerry Abershaw.	Mrs. Brierly's Niece.
Blood Money: A Tale.	Society: A Novel."

The time was out of joint; but Stevenson was born to set it right. Not seven years after the posting of this letter, the recent Romantic Revival had begun. In the year of his death, 1894, it was in full swing; everybody was reading not only Stevenson, but *The Prisoner of Zenda, A Gentleman of France, Under the Red Robe,* etc. Whatever we may think of the literary quality of some of these then popular stories, there is no doubt that the change was in many ways beneficial, and that the influence of Stevenson was more responsible for it than that of any other one man. This was everywhere recognised: in the *Athenæum* for 22 December, 1894, a critic remarked, "The Romantic Revival in the English novel of to-day had in him its leader. . . . But for him they might have been Howells and

James young men." As a germinal writer, Stevenson will always occupy an important place in the history of English prose fiction. And seldom has a man been more conscious of his mission.

Stevenson's high standing as an English classic depends very largely on the excellence of his literary style, although Scott and Cooper won immortality without it. (One wonders if they could to-day.) When some fifteen years ago a few critics had the temerity to suggest that he was equal, if not superior, to these worthies, it sounded like blasphemy; but such an opinion is not uncommon now, and may be reasonably defended. Stevenson lacked in some degree the virility and the astonishing fertility of invention possessed by Scott; but he exhibited a technical skill undreamed of by his great predecessor. From the prefatory verses to *Treasure Island*, we know that he admired Cooper; and he loved Sir Walter, without being in the least blind to his faults. "It is undeniable that the love of the slap-dash and the shoddy grew upon Scott with success." He " had not only splendid romantic, but splendid tragic, gifts. How comes it, then, that he could so often fob us off with languid, inarticulate twaddle?... He was a great day-dreamer, a seer of fit and beautiful and humorous visions, but hardly a great artist; hardly, in the manful sense, an artist at all." Stevenson seems to have felt that Scott's deficiencies in style were not merely artistic, but moral; he lacked the patience and the particular kind of industry required. Scott loved to tell a good story, but he loved the story better than he did the telling of it; Stevenson, on the other hand, was fully as much absorbed by the manner of narration as by the narration itself. Stevenson was keenly alive to the fact that writers of romances did not seem to feel the necessity of style; whereas those who wrote novels wherein nothing happened, felt that a good style atoned for both the lack of incident and the lack of ideas. Stevenson's articles of literary faith apparently included the dogma that a mysterious, blood-curdling romance had fully as much dignity as a minute examination of the dreary, common-place life of the submerged; and that the former made just as high a demand on the endowment and industry of a master-artist. If he had had not an idea in his head, he could not have written with more elegance.

There is, of course, some truth in the charge that Stevenson was not only a master of style, but a stylist. He is indeed something of a macaroni in words; occasionally he struts a bit, and he loves to show his brilliant plumes. He performed dexterous tricks with language, like a musician with a difficult instrument. He liked style for its own sake, and was not averse to exhibiting his technique.

In a slight degree, his attitude and his influence in mere composition are somewhat similar to those of John Lyly three hundred years before. Lyly delighted his readers with unexpected quips and quiddities, with a fantastic display of rhetoric; he showed, as no one had before him, the possible flexibility of English prose. There is more than a touch of Euphuism in Stevenson; he was never insincere, but he was consciously fine. Many have swallowed without salt his statement that he learned to write by imitation; that by the "sedulous ape" method, employed with unwearying study of great models, he himself became a successful author. Men of genius are never to be trusted when they discuss the origin and development of their powers; it is no more to be believed that Stevenson learned to be a great writer by imitating Browne, than that *The Raven* really reached its perfection in the manner so minutely described by Poe. The faithful practice of composition will doubtless help any ambitious young man or woman. But Stevensons are not made in that fashion. If they were, anyone with plenty of time and patience could become a great author. This "ape" remark by Stevenson has had one interesting effect; if he imitated others, he has been strenuously imitated himself. Probably no recent English writer has been more constantly employed for rhetorical purposes, and there is none whose influence on style is more evident in the work of contemporary aspirants in fiction.

The stories of Stevenson exhibit a double union, as admirable as it is rare. They exhibit the union of splendid material with the most delicate skill in language; and they exhibit the union of thrilling events with a remarkable power of psychological analysis. Every thoughtful reader has noticed these combinations; but we sometimes forget that Silver, Alan, Henry, and the Master are just as fine examples of character-portrayal as can be found in the works of Henry James. It is from this point of view that Stevenson is so vastly superior to Fenimore Cooper; just as in literary style he so far surpasses Scott. *Treasure Island* is much better than *The Red Rover* or *The Pirate;* its author actually beat Scott and Cooper at their own game. With the exception of *Henry Esmond,* Stevenson may perhaps be said to have written the best romances in the English language; the undoubted inferiority of any of his books to that masterpiece would make an interesting subject for reflexion.

The one thing in which Scott really excelled Stevenson was in the depiction of women. The latter has given us no Diana Vernon or Jeannie Deans. For the most part, Stevenson's romances are Paradise before the creation of Eve. The snake is there, but not the woman. This extraordinary

absence of sex-interest is a notable feature, and many
have been the reasons assigned for it. If he had not
tried at all, we should be safe in saying that, like
a small boy, he felt that girls were in the way, and
he did not want them mussing up his games. There
is perhaps some truth in this; for the presence of
a girl might have ruined *Treasure Island*, as it
ruined the *Sea Wolf*. Her fuss and feathers bring
in all sorts of bothersome problems to distract a
novelist, bent on having a good time with pirates,
murders, and hidden treasure. Unfortunately for
the complete satisfaction of this explanation, Stevenson wrote *Prince Otto*, and tried to draw a real woman.
The result did not add anything to his fame, and,
indeed, the whole book missed fire. He was unquestionably more successful in *David Balfour*, but,
when all is said, the presence of women in a few of
Stevenson's romances is not so impressive as their
absence in most. It is only in that unfinished work,
Weir of Hermiston, which gave every promise of
being one of the greatest novels in English literature,
that he seemed to have reached full maturity of
power in dealing with the master passion. The best
reason for Stevenson's reserve on matters of sex was
probably his delicacy; he did not wish to represent
this particular animal impulse with the same vivid
reality he pictured avarice, ambition, courage,
cowardice, and pride; and thus hampered by con-

science, he thought it best in the main to omit it altogether. At least, this is the way he felt about it, as we may learn from the *Vailima Letters:* —

"This is a poison bad world for the romancer, this Anglo-Saxon world; I usually get out of it by not having any women in it at all." (February, 1892.)

"I am afraid my touch is a little broad in a love story; I can't mean one thing and write another. As for women, I am no more in any fear of them; I can do a sort all right; age makes me less afraid of a petticoat, but I am a little in fear of grossness. However, this David Balfour's love affair, that's all right — might be read out to a mothers' meeting — or a daughters' meeting. The difficulty in a love yarn, which dwells at all on love, is the dwelling on one string; it is manifold, I grant, but the root fact is there unchanged, and the sentiment being very intense, and already very much handled in letters, positively calls for a little pawing and gracing. With a writer of my prosaic literalness and pertinency of point of view, this all shoves toward grossness — positively even towards the far more damnable *closeness*. This has kept me off the sentiment hitherto, and now I am to try: Lord! Of course Meredith can do it, and so could Shakespeare; but with all my romance, I am a realist and a prosaist, and a most fanatical lover of plain physical sensations plainly and expressly rendered; hence my perils. To do love in the same spirit as I did (for instance) D. Balfour's fatigue in the heather; my dear sir, there were grossness — ready made! And hence, how to sugar?" (May, 1892.)

On the whole, I am inclined to think, that with the omission of the fragment, *Weir of Hermiston,* Stevenson's best novel is his first — *Treasure Island.*

He wrote this with peculiar zest; first of all, in spite of the playful dedication, to please himself; second, to see if the public appetite for Romance could once more be stimulated. He never did anything later quite so off-hand, quite so spontaneous. His maturer books, brilliant as they are, lack the peculiar *brightness* of *Treasure Island*. It has more unity than *The Master of Ballantræ;* and it has a greater group of characters than *Kidnapped*.

Stevenson told this story in the first person, but, by a clever device, he avoided the chief difficulty of that method of narration. The speaker is not one of the principal characters in the story, though he shares in the most thrilling adventures. We thus have all the advantages of direct discourse, all the gain in reality — without a hint as to what will be the fate of the leading actors. Stevenson said, in one of the *Vailima Letters*, that first-person tales were more in accord with his temperament. The purely objective character of this novel is noteworthy, and entirely proper, coming from a perfectly normal boy. The *Essays* show that Stevenson could be sufficiently introspective if he chose, and *Dr. Jekyll* is really an introspective novel, differing in every way from *Treasure Island*. But here we have romantic adventures seen through the fresh eyes of boyhood, producing their unconscious reflex action on the soul of the narrator, who daily grows in courage and self-reliance by grappling with danger. In Henry James's fine and penetrating essay on Stevenson, he says of this book, "What we see in it is not only the ideal fable, but the young reader himself and his state of mind: we seem to read it over his shoulder, with an arm around his neck." This particular remark has been much praised; but it seems in a way to half-apologise for a man's interest in the story, and to explain it like an affectionate uncle's sympathetic interest in a child's game, who mainly enjoys the child's enthusiasm. Now I venture to say that no one can any more outgrow *Treasure Island* than he can outgrow *Robinson Crusoe*. The events in the story delight children; but it is a book that in mature years can be read and reread with ever increasing satisfaction and profit. No one needs to regret or to explain his interest in this novel; it is nothing to be sorry for, nor does it indicate a low order of literary taste. Many serious persons have felt somewhat alarmed by their pleasure in reading *Treasure Island*, and have hesitated to assign it a high place in fiction. Some have said that, after all, it is only a pirate story, differing from the Sleuths and Harkaways merely in being better written. But this is exactly the point, and a very important point, in criticism. In art, the subject is of comparatively little importance, whereas the treatment is the absolute distinguishing feature. To insist that there is little difference between *Treasure Island* and any cheap tale of blood-and-thunder, is equivalent to saying that there is little difference between the Sistine Madonna and a cottage chromo of the Virgin.

Pew is a fearsome personage, and a notable example of the triumph of mind over the most serious of all physical disabilities. Theoretically, it seems strange that able-bodied individuals should be afraid of a man who is stone blind. But the appearance of Pew is enough to make anybody take to his heels. He is the very essence of authority and leadership. The tap-tapping of his stick in the moonlight makes one's blood run cold. We are apt to think of blind people as gentle, sweet, pure, and holy; made submissive and tender by misfortune, dependent on the kindness of others. Old Pew has lost his eyes, but not his nerve. To see so black-hearted and unscrupulous a villain, his sight taken away as it were by the hand of God, and yet intent only on desperate wickedness, upsets the moral order; he becomes an uncanny monstrosity; he takes on the hue of a supernatural fiend. John Silver has lost a leg, but he circumvents others by the speed of his mind; amazingly quick in perception, a most astute politician, arrested from no treachery or murder by any moral principle or touch of pity, he has the dark splendour of unflinching depravity. He is no Laodicean. He never lets I dare not wait upon I would. His course seems fickle and changeable, but he is really steering steadily by the compass of self-interest. He can be witty, affectionate, sympathetic, friendly, submissive, flattering, and also a devilish beast. He is the very chameleon of crime. Stevenson simply had not the heart to kill so consummate an artist in villainy. It was no mean achievement to create two heroes so sinister as Pew and Silver, while depriving one of his sight and the other of a leg. One wearies of the common run of romances, where the chief character is a man of colossal size and beautifully proportioned, so that his victories over various rascals are really only athletic records. In *Treasure Island*, the emphasis is laid in the right place, whence leadership comes; everybody is afraid of Long John, and nobody minds Ben Gunn, dead or alive.[1]

There are scenes in this story, presented with such dramatic power, and with such astonishing felicity of diction, that, once read, they can never pass from the reader's mind. The expression in Silver's face, as he talks with Tom in the marsh, first ingratiatingly friendly, then suspicious, then

[1] It is interesting to remember that the crippled poet, W. E. Henley, was the original of Silver. Writing to Henley, May, 1883, Stevenson said, "I will now make a confession. It was the sight of your maimed strength and masterfulness that begot John Silver."

as implacable as malignant fate. The hurling of the crutch; the two terrific stabs of the knife. "I could hear him pant aloud as he struck the blows." The boy's struggle on the schooner with Israel Hands; the awful moment in the little boat, while Flint's gunner is training the "long nine" on her, and the passengers can do nothing but await the result of the enemy's skill; the death of the faithful old servant, Redruth, who said he thought somebody might read a prayer.

Much has been written in both prose and verse of the fascination of Stevenson's personality. He was so different in different moods that no two of his friends have ever agreed as to what manner of man he really was. As he chose to express his genius mainly in objective romances, future generations will find in the majority of his works no hint as to the character of the author. From this point of view, compare for a moment *The Master of Ballantræ* with *Joseph Vance!* But fortunately, Stevenson elected to write personal essays; and still more fortunately, hundreds of his most intimate letters are preserved in type. Some think that these *Letters* form his greatest literary work, and that they will outlast his novels, plays, poems, and essays. For they will have a profound interest long after the last person who saw Stevenson on earth has passed away. They are the revelation of a man even more interesting than any of the wonderful characters he created; they show that men like Philip Sidney were as possible in the nineteenth century as in the brilliant age of Elizabeth. The life of Stevenson has added immensely to our happiness and enjoyment of the world, and no literary figure in recent times had more radiance and wholesome charm. His optimism was based on a chronic experience of physical pain and weakness; to him it was a good world, and he made it distinctly better by his presence. He was a combination of the Bohemian and the Covenanter; he had all the graces of one, and the bed-rock moral earnestness of the other. "The world must return some day to the word 'duty,'" said he, "and be done with the word 'reward.'" He was the incarnation of the happy union of virtue and vivacity.

X

MRS. HUMPHRY WARD

It is high time that somebody spoke out his mind about Mrs. Humphry Ward. Her prodigious vogue is one of the most extraordinary literary phenomena of our day. A roar of approval greets the publication of every new novel from her active pen, and it is almost pathetic to contemplate the reverent awe of her army of worshippers when they behold the solemn announcement that she is "collecting material" for another masterpiece. Even professional reviewers lose all sense of proportion when they discuss her books, and their so-called criticisms sound like publishers' advertisements. Sceptics are warned to remain silent, lest they become unpleasantly conspicuous. When *Lady Rose's Daughter* appeared, the critic of a great metropolitan daily remarked that whoever did not immediately recognise the work as a masterpiece thereby proclaimed himself as a person incapable of judgement, taste, and appreciation. This is a fair example of the attitude taken by thousands of her readers, and it is this attitude, rather than the value of her work, that we must, first of all, consider.

In the year 1905 an entirely respectable journal said of Mrs. Ward, "There is no more interesting and important figure in the literary world to-day." In comparing this superlative with the actual state of affairs, we find that we were asked to believe that Mrs. Ward was a literary personage not second in importance to Tolstoi, Ibsen, Björnson, Heyse, Sudermann, Hauptmann, Anatole France, Jules Lemaître, Rostand, Swinburne, Thomas Hardy, Meredith, Kipling, and Mark Twain. At about the same time a work appeared intended as a text-book for the young, which declared Mrs. Ward to be "the greatest living writer of fiction in English literature," and misspelled her name — an excellent illustration of carelessness in adjectives with in-accuracy in facts. Over and over again we have heard the statement that the "mantle" of George Eliot has fallen on Mrs. Ward. Is it really true that her stories are equal in value to *Adam Bede*, *The Mill on the Floss*, and *Middlemarch*?

The object of this essay is not primarily to attack a dignified and successful author; it is rather to enquire, in a proper spirit of humility, and with a full realisation of the danger incurred, whether or not the actual output justifies so enormous a repu-tation. For in some respects I believe the vogue of Mrs. Ward to be more unfortunate than the vogue of the late lamented Duchess, of Laura Jean Libbey, of Mrs. E. D. E. N. Southworth, of Marie Corelli, and of Hall Caine. When we are asked to note that 300,000 copies of the latest novel by any of these have been sold before the book is published, there is no cause for alarm. We know perfectly well what that means. It is what is called a "business proposition"; it has nothing to do with literature. It simply proves that it is possible to make as splendid a fortune out of the trade of book-making, and by equally respectable methods, as is made in other legitimate avenues of business. But the case is quite different with Mrs. Ward. Whatever she is, she is not vulgar, sensational, or cheap; she has never made the least compromise with her moral ideals, nor has she ever attempted to play to the gallery. Her constituency is made up largely of serious-minded, highly respectable people, who live in good homes, who are fairly well read, and who ought to know the difference between ordinary and extraordinary literature. Her books have had a bad effect in blurring this distinction in the popular mind; for while she has never written a positively bad book, — with the possible exception of *Bessie Costrell*, — I feel confident that she has never written supremely well; that, compared with the great masters of fiction, she becomes immediately insignificant. If there ever was a successful writer whose work shows industry and talent rather than genius, that writer is Mrs. Ward. If there ever was a successful writer whose work is ordinary rather than extraordinary, it is Mrs. Ward.

To those of us who delight in getting some enjoyment even out of the most depressing facts, the growth of Mrs. Ward's reputation has its humorous aspect. The same individuals (mostly feminine) who in 1888 read *Robert Elsmere* with dismay, who thought the sale of the work should be prohibited, and the copies already purchased removed from circulating libraries, are the very same ones who now worship what they once denounced. She was then regarded as a destroyer of Christian faith. Well, if she was Satan then, she is Satan still (one Western clergyman, in advocating at that time the suppression of the work, said he believed in hitting the devil right between the eyes). She has given no sign of recantation, or even of penitence. I remember one fond mother, who, fearful of the effect of the book on her daughter's growing mind, marked all the worst passages, and then told Alice she might read it, provided she skipped all the blazed places! That indicated not only a fine literary sense, but a remarkable knowledge of human nature. I wonder what the poor girl did when she came to the danger signals! And, as a matter of fact, how valuable or vital would a Christian faith be that could be destroyed by the perusal of *Robert Elsmere*? It is almost difficult now to bring to distinct recollection the tremendous excitement caused by Mrs. Ward's first successful novel, for it is a long time since I heard its name mentioned. The last public notice of it that I can recall was a large sign which appeared some fifteen years ago in a New Haven apothecary's window to the effect that one copy of *Robert Elsmere* would be presented free to each purchaser of a cake of soap!

Although *Robert Elsmere* was an immediate and prodigious success, and made it certain that whatever its author chose to write next would be eagerly bought, it is wholly untrue to say that her subsequent novels have depended in any way on *Elsmere* for their reputation. There are many instances in professional literary careers where one immensely successful book — *Lorna Doone*, for example — has floated a long succession of works that could not of themselves stay above water; many an author has succeeded in attaching a life-preserver to literary children who cannot swim. Far otherwise is the case with Mrs. Ward. It is probable that over half the readers of *Diana Mallory* have never seen a copy of *Robert Elsmere*, for which, incidentally, they are to be congratulated. But many of us can easily recollect with what intense eagerness the novel that followed that sensation was awaited.

Every one wondered if it would be equally good; and many confidently predicted that she had shot her bolt. As a matter of fact, not only was *David Grieve* a better novel than *Robert Elsmere*, but, in my judgement, it is the best book its author has ever written. Oscar Wilde said that *Robert Elsmere* was *Literature and Dogma* with the literature left out. Now, *David Grieve* has no dogma at all, but in a certain sense it does belong to literature. It has some actual dynamic quality. The character of David, and its development in a strange environment, are well analysed; and altogether the best thing in the work, taken as a whole, is the perspective. It is a difficult thing to follow a character from childhood up, within the pages of one volume, and have anything like the proper perspective. It requires for one thing, hard, painstaking industry; but Mrs. Ward has never been afraid of work. She cannot be accused of laziness or carelessness. The ending of this book is, of course, weak, like the conclusion of all her books, for she has never learned the fine art of saying farewell, either to her characters or to the reader.

It was in the year 1894 — a year made memorable by the appearance of *Trilby*, the *Prisoner of Zenda*, *The Jungle Book*, *Lord Ormont and his Aminta*, *Esther Waters*, and other notable novels — that Mrs. Ward greatly increased her reputation and widened

her circle of readers by the publication of *Marcella.*
Here she gave us a political-didactic-realistic novel,
which she has continued to publish steadily ever
since under different titles. It was gravely announced
that this new book would deal with socialism and
the labour question. Many readers, who felt that
she had said the last word on agnosticism in *Elsmere,*
now looked forward with reverent anticipation not
only to the final solution of socialistic problems, but
to some coherent arrangement of their own vague
and confused ideas. Naturally, they got just what
they deserved — a voluminous statement of various
aspects of the problem, with no solution at all. It
is curious how many persons suppose that their
favourite author or orator has done something toward settling questions, when, as a matter of fact,
all he has done is to *state* them, and then state them
again. This is especially true of philosophical
and metaphysical difficulties. Think how eagerly
readers took up Professor James's exceedingly clever
book on Pragmatism, hoping at last to find rest in
some definite principle. And if there ever was a
blind alley in philosophy, it is Pragmatism — the
very essence of agnosticism.

Now, *Marcella,* as a document, is both radical
and reactionary. There is an immense amount of
radical talk; but the heroine's schemes fail, the
Labour party is torn by dissension, Wharton proves

to be a scoundrel, and the rebel Marcella marries a respectable nobleman. There is not a single page in the book, with all its wilderness of words, that can be said to be in any sense a serious contribution to the greatest of all purely political problems. And, as a work of art, it is painfully limited; but since it has the same virtues and defects of all her subsequent literary output, we may consider what these virtues and defects are.

In the first place, Mrs. Ward is totally lacking in one almost fundamental quality of the great novelist — a keen sense of humour. Who are the English novelists of the first class? They are Defoe, Richardson, Fielding, Scott, Jane Austen, Dickens, Thackeray, George Eliot, Stevenson, and perhaps Hardy. Every one of these shows humour enough and to spare, with the single exception of Richardson, and he atoned for the deficiency by a terrible intensity that has seldom, if ever, been equalled in English fiction. Now, the absence of humour in a book is not only a positive loss to the reader, in that it robs him of the fun which is an essential part of the true history of any human life, and thereby makes the history to that extent inaccurate and unreal, but the writer who has no humour seldom gets the right point of view. There is infinitely more in the temperament of the humorist than mere laughter. Just as the poet sees life through the medium of a splendid imagination, so the humorist has the almost infallible guide of sympathy. The humorist sees life in a large, tolerant, kindly way; he knows that life is a tragi-comedy, and he makes the reader feel it in that fashion.

Again, the lack of humour in a writer destroys the sense of proportion. The humorist sees the salient points — the merely serious writer gives us a mass of details. In looking back over the thousands of pages of fiction that Mrs. Ward has published, how few great scenes stand out bright in the memory! The principle of selection — so important a part of all true art — is conspicuous only by its absence. This is one reason for the sameness of her books. All that we can remember is an immense number of social functions and an immense amount of political gossip — a long, sad level of mediocrity. This perhaps helps to explain why German fiction is so markedly inferior to the French. The German, in his scientific endeavour to get in the whole of life, gives us a mass of unrelated detail. A French writer by a few phrases makes us see a character more clearly than a German presents him after many painful pages of wearisome description.

Mrs. Ward is not too much in earnest in following her ideals of art; no one can be. But she is too sadly serious. There is a mental tension in her books, like the tension of overwork and mental exhaustion, like the tension of overwrought nerves; her books are, in fact, filled with tired and over-worked men and women, jaded and gone stale. How many of her characters seem to need a change — what they want is rest and sleep! Many of them ought to be in a sanatorium.

Her books are devoid of charm. One does not have to compare her with the great masters to feel this deficiency; it would not be fair to compare her with Thackeray. But if we select among all the novelists of real distinction the one whom, perhaps, she most closely approaches, — Anthony Trollope, — the enormous distance between *Diana Mallory* and *Framley Parsonage* is instantly manifest. We think of Trollope with a glow of reminiscent delight; but although Trollope and Mrs. Ward talk endlessly on much the same range of subject-matter, how far apart they really are! Mrs. Ward's books are crammed with politicians and clergymen, who keep the patient reader informed on modern aspects of political and religious thought; but the difficulty is that they substitute phrases for ideas. Mrs. Ward knows all the political and religious cant of the day; she is familiar with the catch-words that divide men into hostile camps; but in all these dreary pages of serious conversation there is no real illumi-nation. She completely lacks the art that Trollope possessed, of making ordinary people attractive.

But to find out the real distance that separates her productions from literature, one should read, let us say, *The Marriage of William Ashe* and then take up *Pride and Prejudice.* The novels of Mrs. Ward bear about the same relation to first-class fiction that maps and atlases bear to great paintings.

This lack of charm that I always feel in reading Mrs. Ward's books (and I have read them all) is owing not merely to the lack of humour. It is partly due to what seems to be an almost total absence of freshness, spontaneity, and originality. Mrs. Ward works like a well-trained and high-class graduate student, who is engaged in the preparation of a doctor's thesis. Her discussions of socialism, her scenes in the House of Commons and on the Terrace, her excursions to Italy, her references to political history, her remarks on the army, her disquisitions on theology, her pictures of campaign riots, her studies of defective drainage, her representations of the labouring classes, — all these are "worked up" in a scholarly and scientific manner; there is the modern passion for accuracy, there is the German completeness of detail, — there is, in fact, everything except the breath of life. She works in the descriptive manner, from the outside in — not in the inspired manner which goes with imagination, sympathy, and genius. She is not only a student, she is a journalist; she is a special correspondent on politics and theology; but she is not a creative writer. For she has the critical, not the creative, temperament.

The monotonous sameness of her books, which has been mentioned above, is largely owing to the sameness of her characters. She changes the frames, but not the portraits. First of all, in almost any of her books we are sure to meet the studious, intellectual young man. He always has a special library on some particular subject, with the books all annotated. One wearies of this perpetual character's perpetual library, crowded, as it always is, with the latest French and German monographs. Her heroes smell of books and dusty dissertations, and the conversations of these heroes are plentifully lacking in native wit and originality — they are the mere echoes of their reading. Let us pass in review a few of these serious students — Robert Elsmere, Langham, Aldous Reyburn (who changes into Lord Maxwell, but who remains a prig), the melancholy Helbeck, the insufferable Manisty, Jacob Delafield, William Ashe, Oliver Marsham — all, all essentially the same, tiresome, dull, heavy men — what a pity they were not intended as satires! Second, as a foil to this man, we have the Byronic, clever, romantic, sentimental, insincere man — who always degenerates or dies in a manner that exalts the dull and superior virtues of his antagonist. Such a man is Wharton, or Sir George Tressady, or Captain Warkworth, or Cliffe — they have different names in different novels, but they are the same character. Curiously enough, the only convincing men that appear in her pages are *old* men — men like Lord Maxwell or Sir James Chide. In portraying this type she achieves success.

What shall we say of her heroines? They have the same suspicious resemblance so characteristic of her heroes; they are represented as physically beautiful, intensely eager for morality and justice, with an extraordinary fund of information, and an almost insane desire to impart it. Her heroine is likely to be or to become a power in politics; even at a tender age she rules society by the brilliancy of her conversation; in a crowded drawing-room the Prime Minister hangs upon her words; diplomats are amazed at her intimate knowledge of foreign relations, and of the resources of the British Empire; and she can entertain a whole ring of statesmen and publicists by giving to each exactly the right word at the right moment. Men who are making history come to her not only for inspiration but for guidance, for she can discourse fluently on all phases of the troublesome labour question. And yet, if we may judge of this marvellous creature not by the attitude of the other characters in the book, but by the actual words that fall from her lips, we are reminded of the woman whom Herbert Spencer's friends selected as his potential spouse. They shut him up with her, and awaited the result with eagerness, for they told him she had a great mind; but on emerging from the trial interview Spencer remarked that she would not do at all: "The young lady is, in my opinion, too highly intellectual; or, I should rather say — morbidly intellectual. A small brain in a state of intense activity." Was there ever a better formula for Mrs. Ward's constantly recurring heroine? Now, as a foil to Marcella, Diana Mallory, and the others, Mrs. Ward gives us the frivolous, mischief-making, would-be brilliant, and actually vulgar woman, who makes much trouble for the heroine and ultimately more for herself — the wife of Sir George Tressady, the young upstart in *Diana Mallory*, and all the rest of them. By the introduction of these characters there is an attempt to lend colour to the dull pages of the novels. These women are at heart adventuresses, but they are apt to lack the courage of their convictions; instead of being brilliant and terrible, — like the great adventuresses of fiction, — they are as dull in sin as their antagonists are dull in virtue. Mrs. Ward cannot make them real; compare any one of them with Thackeray's Beatrix or with Becky Sharp — to say nothing of the long list of sinister women in French and Russian fiction.

There are no "supreme moments" in Mrs. Ward's books; no great dramatic situations; she has tried hard to manage this, for she has had repeatedly one eye on the stage. When *The Marriage of William Ashe* and *Lady Rose's Daughter* appeared, one could almost feel the strain for dramatic effect. It was as though she had realised that her previous books were treatises rather than novels, and had gathered all her energies together to make a severe effort for real drama. But, unfortunately, the scholarly and critical temperament is not primarily adapted for dramatic masterpieces. In the endeavour to recall thrilling scenes in her novels, scenes that brand themselves for ever on the memory, one has only to compare her works with such stories as *Far From the Madding Crowd* or *The Return of the Native*, and her painful deficiency is immediately apparent.

In view of what I believe to be the standard mediocrity of her novels, how shall we account for their enormous vogue? The fact is, whether we like it or not, that she is one of the most widely read of all living novelists. Well, in the first place, she is absolutely respectable and safe. It is assuredly to her credit that she has never stooped for popularity. She has never descended to melodrama, clap-trap, or indecency. She is never spectacular and declamatory like Marie Corelli, and she is never morally offensive like some popular writers who might be mentioned. She writes for a certain class of readers whom she thoroughly understands: they are the readers who abhor both vulgarity and pruriency, and who like to enter vicariously, as they certainly do in her novels, into the best English society. In her social functions her readers can have the pleasure of meeting prime ministers, lords, and all the dwellers in Mayfair, and they know that nothing will be said that is shocking or improper. Her books can safely be recommended to young people, and they reflect the current movement of English thought as well as could be done by a standard English review. She has a well-furnished and highly developed intellect; she is deeply read; she makes her readers think that they are thinking. She tries to make up for artistic deficiencies by an immense amount of information. Fifty years ago it is probable that she would not have written novels at all, but rather thoughtful and intellectual critical essays, for which her mind is admirably fitted. She unconsciously chose the novel simply because the novel has been, during the last thirty years, the chief channel of literary expression. But in spite of her popularity, it should never be forgotten that the novel is an art-form, not a medium for doctrinaires.

Then, with her sure hand on the pulse of the public, she is always intensely modern, intensely contemporary; again like a well-trained journalist. She knows exactly what Society is talking about, for she emphatically belongs to it. This is once more a reason why so many people believe that she holds the key to great problems of social life, and that her next book will give the solution. Many hoped that her novel on America, carefully worked up during her visit here, would give the final word on American social life. Both England and the United States were to find out what the word "American" really means.

Mrs. Ward is an exceedingly talented, scholarly, and thoughtful woman, of lofty aims and actuated only by noble motives; she is hungry for intellectual food, reading both old texts and the daily papers with avidity. She has a highly trained, sensitive, critical mind, — but she is destitute of the divine spark of genius. Her books are the books of to-day, not of to-morrow; for while the political and religious questions of to-day are of temporary interest, the themes of the world's great novels are what Richardson called "love and nonsense, men and women" — and these are eternal.

XI

RUDYARD KIPLING

MR. RUDYARD KIPLING is in the anomalous and fortunate position of having enjoyed a prodigious reputation for twenty years, and being still a young man. Few writers in the world to-day are better known than he; and it is to be hoped and expected that he has before him over thirty years of active production. He has not yet attained the age of forty-five; but his numerous stories, novels, and poems have reached the unquestioned dignity of "works," and in uniform binding they make on my library shelves a formidable and gallant display. Foreigners read them in their own tongues; critical essays in various languages are steadily accumulating; and he has received the honour of being himself the hero of a strange French novel.[1] His popularity with the general mass of readers has been sufficient to satisfy the wildest dreams of an author's ambition; and his fame is, in a way, officially sanctioned by the receipt of honorary degrees from McGill University, from Durham, from Oxford, and from Cambridge;

[1] A curious and ironical book, *Dingley*, by Tharaud.

and in 1907 he was given the Nobel Prize, with the
ratifying applause of the whole world.   There is
no indication that either the shouts of the mob or
the hoods of Doctorates have turned his head; he
remains to-day what he always has been — a hard,
conscientious workman, trying to do his best every
time.

Although Mr. Kipling is British to the core, there
is nothing insular about his experience; he is as
much-travelled as Ulysses.

> "For always roaming with a hungry heart
> Much have I seen and known: cities of men,
> And manners, climates, councils, governments,
> Myself not least, but honour'd of them all."

Born in India, educated at an English school, cir-
cumnavigator of the globe, he is equally at home
in the snows of the Canadian Rockies, or in the
fierce heat east of Suez; in the fogs of the Channel,
or under the Southern Cross at Capetown.   Nor is
he a mere sojourner on the earth: he has lived for
years in his own house, in England, in Vermont, and
in India, and has had abundant opportunity to
compare the climate of Brattleboro with that of
Bombay.

A born journalist and reporter, his publications
first saw the light in ephemeral Indian sheets.   In
the late eighties he began to amuse himself with the
composition of squibs of verse, which he printed in

the local newspaper; these became popular, and were cited and sung with enthusiasm. Emboldened by this first taste of success, he put together a little volume bound like a Government report; he then sent around reply post-cards for cash orders, in the fashion already made famous by Walt Whitman. It is needless to say that copies of this book command a fancy price to-day. He immediately contracted what Holmes used to call "lead-poisoning," and the sight of his work in type made a literary career certain. He produced volume after volume, in both prose and verse, with amazing rapidity, and his fame overflowed the world. A London periodical prophesied in 1888, "The book gives hope of a new literary star of no mean magnitude rising in the East." The amount and excellence of his output may be judged when we remember that in the three years from 1886 to 1889 he published *Departmental Ditties, Plain Tales from the Hills, Soldiers Three, In Black and White, The Story of the Gadsbys, The Man Who Would Be King, The Phantom 'Rickshaw, Wee Willie Winkie,* and other narratives.

The originality, freshness, and power of all this work made Europe stare and gasp. For some years he had as much notoriety as reputation. We used to hear of the Kipling "craze," the Kipling "boom," the Kipling "fad," and Kipling clubs sprang up like mushrooms. It was difficult to read him in cool blood, because he was discussed pro and con with so much passion. He was fashionable, in the manner of ping-pong; and there were not wanting pessimistic prophets who looked upon him as a comet rather than a fixed star. So late as 1895 a well-known American journal said of him: "Rudyard Kipling is supposed to be the cleverest man now handling the pen. The magazines accept everything he writes, and pay him fabulous prices. Kipling is now printing a series of Jungle Stories that are so weak and foolish that we have never been able to read them. They are not fables: they are stories of animals talking, and they are pointless, so far as the average reader is able to judge. We have asked a good many magazine editors about Kipling's Jungle Stories; they all express the same astonishment that the magazine editors accept them. Kipling will soon be dropped by the magazine editors; they will inevitably discover that his stories are not admired by the people. Robert Louis Stevenson died just in time to save him from the same fate."

Many honestly believed that Mr. Kipling could write only in flashes; that he was incapable of producing a complete novel. His answer to this was *The Light that Failed*, which, although he made the mistake of giving it a reversible ending, indicated that his own lamp had yet sufficient oil. In 1895 he added immensely to the solidity of his

fame by printing *The Brushwood Boy*, the scenes of
which he announced previously would be laid in
"England, India, and the world of dreams." Here
he temporarily forsook the land of mysterious horror
for the land of mysterious beauty, and many were
grateful, and said so. In 1896 the appearance of
The Seven Seas proved beyond cavil that he was
something more than a music-hall rimester — that
he was really among the English poets. The very
next year *The Recessional* stirred the religious consciousness of the whole English-speaking race.
And although much of his subsequent career seems
to be a nullification of the sentiment of that poem,
it will remain imperishable when the absent-minded
beggars and the flannelled fools have reached the
oblivion they so richly deserve.

In 1897 he tried his hand for the second time at
a complete novel, *Captains Courageous*, and the
result might safely be called a success. The moral
of this story will be worth a word or two later on.
The next year an important volume came from his
pen, *The Day's Work* — important because it is
in this volume that the new Kipling is first plainly
seen, and the mechanical engineer takes the place
of the literary artist. Such curiosities as *The Ship
that Found Herself*, *The Bridge-Builders*, *.007*,
became anything but curiosities in his later work.
This collection was sadly marred by the inclusion

of such wretched stuff as *My Sunday at Home,* and *An Error in the Fourth Dimension;* but it was glorified by one of the most exquisitely tender and beautiful of all Mr. Kipling's tales, *William the Conqueror.* And it should not be forgotten that the author saw fit to close this volume with the previously printed and universally popular *Brushwood Boy.* Then, at the very height of his ten years' fame, Mr. Kipling came closer to death than almost any other individual has safely done. As he lay sick with pneumonia in New York, the American people, whom he has so frequently ridiculed, were more generally and profoundly affected than they have been at the bedside of a dying President. The year 1899 marked the great physical crisis of his life, and seems also to indicate a turning-point in his literary career.

Whatever may be thought of the relative merits of Mr. Kipling's early and later style, it is fortunate for him that the two decades of composition were not transposed. We all read the early work because we could not help it; we read his twentieth-century compositions because he wrote them. It is lucky that the *Plain Tales from the Hills* preceded *Puck of Pook's Hill,* and that *The Light that Failed* came before *Stalky and Co.* Whether these later productions could have got into print without the tremendous prestige of their author's name, is a question that has all the fascination and all the insolubility of speculative philosophy. The suddenness of his early popularity may be perhaps partly accounted for by the fact that he was working a new field. The two authors who have most influenced Mr. Kipling's style are both Americans — Bret Harte and Mark Twain; and the analogy between the sudden fame of Harte and the sudden fame of Mr. Kipling is too obvious to escape notice. Bret Harte found in California ore of a different kind than his maddened contemporaries sought; his early tales had all the charm of something new and strange. What Bret Harte made out of California Mr. Kipling made out of India; at the beginning he was a "sectional writer," who, with the instinct of genius, made his literary opportunity out of his environment. The material was at hand, the time was ripe, and the man was on the spot. It was the strong "local colour" in these powerful Indian tales that captivated readers — who, in far-away centres of culture and comfort, delighted to read of primitive passions in savage surroundings. We had all the rest and change of air that we could have obtained in a journey to the Orient, without any of the expense, discomfort, and peril.

But after the spell of the wizard's imagination has left us, we cannot help asking, after the manner of the small boy, Is it true? Are these pictures of

English and native life in India faithful reflexions of fact? Can we depend on Mr. Kipling for India, as we can depend (let us say) on Daudet for a picture of the *Rue de la Paix?* Now it is a notable fact that local colour seems most genuine to those who are unable to verify it. It is a melancholy truth that the community portrayed by a novelist not only almost invariably deny the likeness of the portrait, but that they emphatically resent the liberty taken. Stories of college life are laughed to scorn by the young gentlemen described therein, no matter how fine the local colour may seem to outsiders. The same is true of social strata in society, of provincial towns, and Heaven only knows what the Slums would say to their depiction in novels, if only the Slums could read. One reason for this is that a novel or a short story must have a beginning and an end, and some kind of a plot; whereas life has no such thing, nor anything remotely resembling it. When honest people see their daily lives, made up of thousands of unrelated incidents, served up to remote readers in the form of an orderly progression of events, leading up to a proper climax, the whole thing seems monstrously unreal and un-true. "Why, we are not in the least like that!" they cry. And I have purposely omitted the factor of exaggeration, absolutely essential to the realistic novelist or playwright.

In a notice of the *Plain Tales from the Hills,* the London *Saturday Review* remarked, "Mr. Kipling knows and appreciates the English in India." But it is more interesting and profitable to see how his stories were regarded in the country he described. In the *Calcutta Times,* for 14 September, 1895, there was a long editorial which is valuable, at any rate, for the point of view. After mentioning the *Plain Tales, Soldiers Three, Barrack-room Ballads,* etc., the *Times* critic said : —

"Except in a few instances which might easily be numbered on the fingers of one hand, nothing in the books we have named is at all likely to live or deserves to live. . . . It will probably be answered that this sweeping condemnation is not of much value against the emphatic approval of the British public and the aforesaid chorus of critics in praise of the new Genius. . . . And the English critics have this to plead in excuse of their hyperbolical appreciation of the Stronger Dickens, that his first work came to them fathered with responsible guarantee from men who should have known better, that it was in the way of a revelation of Anglo-Indian society, a-letting in the light of truth on places which had been very dark indeed.

"Now the average English critic knows very little of the intricacies of social life in India, and in the enthusiasm which Mrs. Hauksbee and kindred creations inspired he accepted too readily as true types what are, in fact, caricatures, or distorted presentments, of some of the more poisonous social characteristics to be found in Anglo-Indian as well as in every other civilised society. . . . Do not let us be understood

as recklessly running down Kipling and all his works. . .
He possesses in a high degree the power of describing a certain
class of emotions, and the flights of his imagination in some
directions are extremely bold and original. In such tales,
for instance, as 'The Man who would be a King' (*sic*) and
'The Ride of Morrowby Jukes' (*sic*) there are qualities of
the imagination which equal, if they do not surpass, anything
in the same line with which we are acquainted. . . . The
capital charge, in the opinion of many, the head and front
of his offending, is that he has traduced a whole society, and
has spread libels broadcast. Anglo-Indian society may in
some respects be below the average level of the best society
in the Western world, where the rush and stir of life and the
collision of intellects combine to keep the atmosphere clearer
and more bracing than in this land of tennis, office boxes,
frontier wars, and enervation. But as far as it falls below
what many would wish it to be, so far it rises above the description of it which now passes current at home under the
sanction of Kipling's name. . . . For whether Kipling is
treating of Indian subjects pure and simple, of Anglo-Indian
subjects, or is attempting a Western theme, the personality
of the writer is pervasive and intrusive everywhere, with all
its limitations of vision and information, as well as with its
eternal panoply of cheap smartness and spiced vulgarity. . . .
Smartness is always first with him, and Truth may shift for
herself."

Although the writer of the above article is somewhat blinded by prejudice and wrath, it is, nevertheless, interesting testimony from the particular
section of our planet which Mr. Kipling was at that
time supposed to know best. And out in San

Francisco they are still talking of Mr. Kipling's visit there, and the "abominable libel" of California life and customs he chose to publish in *From Sea to Sea*.

Apart from Mr. Kipling's good fortune in having fresh material to deal with, the success of his early work lay chiefly in its dominant quality — Force. For the last thirty years, the world has been full of literary experts, professional story-writers, to whom the pen is a means of livelihood. Our magazines are crowded with tales which are well written, and nothing else. They say nothing, because their writers have nothing to say. The impression left on the mind by the great majority of handsomely bound novels is like that of a man who beholds his natural face in a glass. The thing we miss is the thing we unconsciously demand — Vitality. In the rare instances where vitality is the ground-quality, readers forgive all kinds of excrescences and defects, as they did twenty years ago in Mr. Kipling, and later, for example, in Jack London. The original vigour and strength of Mr. Kipling's stories were to the jaded reader a keen, refreshing breeze; like Marlowe in Elizabethan days he seemed a towering, robust, masculine personality, who had at his command an inexhaustible supply of material absolutely new. This undoubted vigour was naturally unaccompanied by moderation and good taste; Mr. Kipling's sins against artistic proportion and the law of subtle suggestion were black indeed. He simply had no reserve. In *The Man Who Would Be King*, which I have always regarded as his masterpiece, the subject was so big that no reserve in handling it was necessary. The whole thing was an inspiration, of imagination all compact. But in many other instances his style was altogether too loud for his subject. One wearies of eternal fortissimo. Many of his tales should have been printed throughout in italics. In examples of this nature, which are all too frequent in the "Complete Works" of Mr. Kipling, the tragedy becomes melodrama; the humour becomes buffoonery; the picturesque becomes bizarre; the terrible becomes horrible; and vulgarity reigns supreme.

He is far better in depicting action than in portraying character. This is one reason why his short stories are better than his novels. In *The Light that Failed*, with all its merits, he never realised the character of Maisie; but in his tales of violent action, we feel the vividness of the scene, time and again. His work here is effective, because Mr. Kipling has an acute sense of the value of words, just as a great musician has a correct ear for the value of pitch. When one takes the trouble to analyse his style in his most striking passages, it all comes down to skill in the use of the specific word — the

word that makes the picture clear, sometimes intolerably clear. Look at the nouns and adjectives
in this selection from *The Drums of the Fore and Aft*:

"They then selected their men, and slew them with deep
gasps and short hacking coughs, and groanings of leather
belts against strained bodies, and realised for the first time
that an Afghan attacked is far less formidable than an Afghan
attacking; which fact old soldiers might have told them.

"But they had no old soldiers in their ranks."

There are two defects in Mr. Kipling's earlier work
that might perhaps be classed as moral deficiencies.
One is the almost ever present coarseness, which the
author mistook for vigour. Now the tendency to
coarseness is inseparable from force, and needs to
be held in check. Coarseness is the inevitable ex-
crescence of superabundant vitality, just as effemi-
nacy is the danger limit of delicacy and refinement.
Swift and Rabelais had the coarseness of a robust
English sailor; at their worst they are simply abominable, just as Tennyson at his worst is effemi-
nate and silly. Mr. Kipling has that natural delight
in coarseness that all strong natures have, whether
they are willing to admit it or not. A large proportion of his scenes of humour are devoted to
drunkenness: "gloriously drunk" is a favourite
phrase with him. The time may come when this
sort of humour will be obsolete. We laugh at
drunkenness, as the Elizabethans laughed at insanity,

but we are only somewhat nearer real civilisation than they. At any rate, even those who delight in scenes of intoxication must find the theme rather overworked in Mr. Kipling. This same defect in him leads to indulgence in his passion for ghastly detail. This is where he ceases to be a man of letters, and becomes downright journalistic. It is easier to excite momentary attention by physical horror than by any other device; and Mr. Kipling is determined to leave nothing to the imagination. Many instances might be cited; we need only recall the gouging out of a man's eye in *The Light that Failed*, and the human brains on the boot in *Badalia Herodsfoot*.

The other moral defect in this early work was its world-weary cynicism, which was simply foolish in so young a writer. His treatment of women, for example, compares unfavourably with that shown in the frankest tales of Bret Harte. His attitude toward women in these youthful books has been well described as "disillusioned gallantry." The author continually gives the reader a "knowing wink," which, after a time, gets on one's nerves. These books, after all, were probably not meant for women to read, and perhaps no one was more surprised than Mr. Kipling himself at the rapturous exclamations of the thousands of his feminine adorers. A woman rejoicing in the perusal of these Indian tales seems as much out of place as she does in the office of a cheap country hotel, reeking with the fumes of whiskey and stale tobacco, and adorned with men who spit with astonishing accuracy into distant receptacles.

Mr. Kipling doubtless knows more about his own faults than any of the critics; and if after one has read *The Light that Failed* for the sake of the story, one rereads it attentively as an *Apologia Pro Vita Sua*, one will be surprised to see how many ideas about his art he has put into the mouth of Dick. "Under any circumstances, remember, four-fifths of everybody's work must be bad. But the remnant is worth the trouble for its own sake." "One must do something always. You hang your canvas up in a palm-tree and let the parrots criticise." "If we sit down quietly to work out notions that are sent to us, we may or we may not do something that isn't bad. A great deal depends on being master of the bricks and mortar of the trade. But the instant we begin to think about success and the effect of our work — to play with one eye on the gallery — we lose power and touch and everything else. . . . I was told that all the world was interested in my work, and everybody at Kami's talked turpentine, and I honestly believed that the world needed elevating and influencing, and all manner of impertinences, by my brushes. By Jove, I actually believed that!

. . . And when it's done it's such a tiny thing, and the world's so big, and all but a millionth part of it doesn't care."

Fortunately, four-fifths of Kipling's work isn't bad. We are safe in ascribing genius to the man who wrote *The Phantom 'Rickshaw*, *The Strange Ride*, *The Man Who Would Be King*, *William the Conqueror*, *The Brushwood Boy*, and *The Jungle Book*. These, and many other tales, to say nothing of his poetry, constitute an astounding achievement for a writer under thirty-five.

But the Kipling of the last ten years is an Imperialist and a Mechanic, rather than a literary man. We need not classify *Stalky and Co.*, except to say that it is probably the worst novel ever written by a man of genius. It is on a false pitch throughout, and the most rasping book of recent times. The only good things in it are the quotations from Browning. The Jingo in Mr. Kipling was released by the outbreak of the South African War, and the author of *The Recessional* forgot everything he had prayed God to remember. He became the voice of the British Empire, and the man who had always ridiculed Americans for bunkum oratory, outscreamed us all. In this imperialistic verse and prose there is not much literature, but there is a great deal of noise, which has occasionally deceived the public; just as an orator is sure of a round of applause if his peroration is shouted at the top of his voice. His recent book, *Puck of Pook's Hill*, is written against the grain; painful effort has supplied the place of the old inspiration, and the simplicity of true art is conspicuous by its absence. Of this volume, *The Athenæum*, in general friendly to Kipling, remarks: "In his new part — the missionary of empire — Mr. Kipling is living the strenuous life. He has frankly abandoned story-telling, and is using his complete and powerful armory in the interest of patriotic zeal." On the other hand, Mr. Owen Wister, whose opinion is valuable, thinks *Puck* "the highest plane that he has ever reached" — a judgement that I record with respect, though to me it is incomprehensible.

Kipling the Mechanic is less useful than an encyclopædia, and not any more interesting. A comic paper describes him as "now a technical expert; at one time a popular writer. This young man was born in India, came to his promise in America, and lost himself in England. His *Plain Tales of the Hills* (*sic*) has been succeeded by *Enigmatical Expositions from the Dark Valleys*. . . . Mr. Kipling has declared that the Americans have never forgiven him for not dying in their country. On the contrary, they have never forgiven him for not having written anything better since he was here than he did before. But while there's Kipling, there's hope."

It is to be earnestly hoped that he will cease describing the machinery of automobiles, ships, locomotives,
and flying air-vessels, and once more look in his heart
and write. His worst enemy is himself. He seems to
be in terror lest he should say something ordinary
and commonplace. He has been so praised for his
originality and powerful imagination, that his later
books give one the impression of a man writing in
the sweat of his face, with the grim determination
to make every sentence a literary event. Such a
tale as *Wireless* shows that the zeal for originality
has eaten him up. One can feel on every page the
straining for effect, and it is as exhausting to read
as it is to watch a wrestling-match, and not nearly
so entertaining. If Mr. Kipling goes on in the vein
of these later years, he may ultimately survive his
reputation, as many a good man has done before
him. I should think even now, when the author
of *Puck of Pook's Hill* turns over the pages of *The
Man Who Would Be King*, he would say with Swift,
"Good God! what a genius I had when I wrote that
book!"

His latest collection of tales, with the significant
title, *Actions and Reactions*, is a particularly welcome volume to those of us who prefer the nineteenth century Kipling to the twentieth. To be
sure, the story *With the Night Mail*, shows the new
mechanical cleverness rather than the old inspira-

tion ; it is both ingenious and ephemeral, and should have remained within the covers of the magazine where it first appeared. Furthermore, *A Deal in Cotton, The Puzzler*, and *Little Foxes* are neither clever nor literary ; they are merely irritating, and remind us of a book we would gladly forget, called *Traffics and Discoveries*. But the first narrative in this new volume, with the caption, *An Habitation Enforced*, is one of the most subtle, charming, and altogether delightful things that Mr. Kipling has ever given us; nor has he ever brought English and American people in conjunction with so much charity and good feeling. I do not think he has previously shown greater psychological power than in this beautiful story. In the second tale, *Garm — A Hostage*, Mr. Kipling joins the ranks of the dog worshippers ; the exploits of this astonishing canine will please all dog-owners, and many others as well. Naturally he has to exaggerate; instead of making his four-footed hero merely intelligent, he makes him noble in reason, infinite in faculty, in apprehension like a god, the paragon of animals. But it is a brilliant piece of work. The last story, *The House Surgeon*, takes us into the world of spirit, whither Mr. Kipling has successfully conducted his readers before. This mysterious domain seems to have a constantly increasing attraction for modern realistic writers, and has enormously enlarged the stock of material for contemporary novelists. The field is the world, yes; but the world is bigger than it used to be, bigger than any boundaries indicated by maps or globes. It would be interesting to speculate just what the influence of all these transcendental excursions will be on modern fiction as an educational force. Mr. Kipling apparently writes with sincere conviction, and in a powerfully impressive manner. The poetic interludes in this volume, like those in *Puck of Pook's Hill*, show that the author's skill in verse has not in the least abated; the lines on *The Power of the Dog* are simply irresistible. It is safe to say that *Actions and Reactions* will react favourably on all unprejudiced readers; and for this relief much thanks. If one wishes to observe the difference between the inspired and the ingenious Mr. Kipling, one has only to read this collection straight through.[1]

Like almost all Anglo-Saxon writers, Mr. Kipling is a moralist, and his gospel is Work. He believes in the strenuous life as a cure-all. He apparently does not agree with Goethe that To Be is greater than To Do. The moral of *Captains Courageous* is the same moral contained in the ingenious bee-hive

[1] I have not discussed a new collection of Mr. Kipling's stories, called *Abaft the Funnel*, consisting of reprints of early fugitive pieces ; because there is not the slightest indication that this book is in any way authorised, or that its publication has the approval of the man who wrote it. Perhaps an authorised edition of it may now become necessary.

story. The unpardonable sin is Idleness. But although Work is good for humanity, it is rather limited as an ideal, and we cannot rate Mr. Kipling very high as a spiritual teacher. God is not always in the wind, or in the earthquake, or in the fire. The day-dreams of men like Stevenson and Thackeray sometimes bear more fruit than the furious energy of Mr. Kipling.

But the consuming ambition of this man, and his honest desire to do his best, will, let us hope, spare him the humiliation of being beaten by his own past. After all, Genius is the rarest article in the world, and one who undoubtedly has it is far more likely to reach the top of the hill than he is to take the road to Danger, which leads into a great wood; or the road to Destruction, which leads into a wide field, full of dark mountains.

XII

"LORNA DOONE"

THE air of Devon and Somerset is full of literary germs. The best advice a London hack could give to a Gigadibs would be *Go west, young man.* The essential thing is to establish a residence south of Bristol, grow old along with Wessex, and inhale the atmosphere. Thousands of reverent pilgrims, on foot, on bicycle, and in automobile, are yearly following the tragic trails of Mr. Hardy's heroines; to a constantly increasing circle of interested observers, Mr. Eden Phillpotts is making the topography of Devon clearer than an ordnance map; if Mrs. Willcocks writes a few more novels like *The Wingless Victory* and *A Man of Genius,* we shall soon all be talking about her — just wait and see; and in the summer season, when soft is the sun, the tops of coaches in North Devon and Somerset are packed with excited Americans, carrying Lornas instead of Baedekers. To the book-loving tourists, every inch of this territory is holy ground.

Yet the author of our favourite romance was not by birth a Wessex man. Mr. Richard D. Black-

more (for, like the creator of *Robinson Crusoe*, his
name is not nearly so well known as his work)
first "saw the light" in Berkshire, the year being
1825. But he was exposed to the Wessex germs
at the critical period of boyhood, actually going to
Blundell's School at Tiverton, a small town in the
heart of Devonshire, fourteen miles north of Exeter,
at the union of Exe and Lowman rivers. To this
same school he sent John Ridd, as we learn in the
second paragraph of the novel: —

"John Ridd, the elder, churchwarden, and overseer, being
a great admirer of learning, and well able to write his name,
sent me, his only son, to be schooled at Tiverton, in the
County of Devon. For the chief boast of that ancient town
(next to its woolen staple) is a worthy grammar-school, the
largest in the west of England, founded and handsomely
endowed in the year 1604 by Master Peter Blundell, of that
same place, clothier."

From this institution young Blackmore proceeded
to Exeter College, Oxford, where he laid the foundations of his English style by taking high rank in the
classics. Like many potential poets and novelists,
he studied law, and was called to the bar in 1852.
But he cared little for the dusty purlieus of the
Middle Temple, and not at all for city life: his
father was a country parson, as it is the fashion for
English fathers of men of letters to be, and the young
man loved the peace and quiet of rural scenery.

He finally made a home at Teddington, in Middle-
sex, and devoted himself to the avocation of fruit-
growing. On this subject he became an authority,
and his articles on gardening were widely read.
Here he died in January, 1900.

His death was mourned by many thousand persons
who never saw him, and who knew nothing about his
life. The public always loves the makers of its
favourite books; but in the case of Mr. Blackmore,
every reader of his masterpiece felt a peculiarly
intimate relation with the man who wrote it. The
story is so full of the milk of human kindness, its
hero and heroine are so irresistibly attractive, and
it radiates so wholesome and romantic a charm,
that one cannot read it without feeling on the best
possible terms with the author — as if both were
intimate friends of long standing. For *Lorna Doone*
is a book we think we have always been reading; we
can hardly recall the time when it had not become
a part of our literary experience; just as it takes an
effort to remember that there were days and years
when we were not even aware of the existence of
persons who are now indissolubly close. They
have since become so necessary that we imagine life
before we knew them must really have been more
barren than it seemed.

Like many successful novelists, Mr. Blackmore
began his literary career by the publication of verse,

several volumes of poems appearing from his pen
during the years 1854–1860. Although he never
entirely abandoned verse composition, which it
was only too apparent that he wrote with his left
hand, the coolness with which his Muse was received
may have been a cause of his attempting the quite
different art of the novel. It is pleasant to remember,
however, that in these early years he translated
Vergil's *Georgics;* combining his threefold love of
the classics, of poetry, and of gardening. Of how
much practical agricultural value he found the
Mantuan bard, we shall never know.

Contrary to a common supposition, *Lorna Doone*
was not his first story. He launched two ventures
before his masterpiece — *Clara Vaughan* in 1864,
and *Cradock Nowell* in 1866. These won no applause, and have not emerged from the congenial
oblivion in which they speedily foundered. After
these false starts, the great book came out in 1869,
with no blare of publisher's trumpet, with scanty
notice from the critics, and with no notice of any kind
from the public. In the preface to the twentieth
edition, and his various prefaces are well worth
reading, the author remarked : —

"What a lucky maid you are, my Lorna ! When first you
came from the Western Moors nobody cared to look at you;
the 'leaders of the public taste' led none of it to make test
of you. Having struggled to the light of day, through ob-

struction and repulses, for a year and a half you shivered in a cold corner, without a sun-ray. Your native land disdained your voice, and America answered, 'No child of mine'; knowing how small your value was, you were glad to get your fare paid to any distant colony."

The *Saturday Review* for 5 November, 1870, uttered a few patronising words of praise. The book was called "a work of real excellence," but the reviewer timidly added, "We do not pretend to rank it with the acknowledged masterpieces of fiction." On the whole, there is good ground for gratitude that the public was so slow to see the "real excellence" of *Lorna*. A sudden blaze of popularity is sometimes so fierce as to consume its cause. Let us spend a few moments in devout meditation, while we recall the ashes of "the book of the year." The gradual dawn of Lorna's fame has assured her of a long and fair day.

Possibly one of the reasons why this great romance made so small an impression was because it appeared at an unpropitious time. The sower sowed the seed; but the thorns of Reade and Trollope sprang up and choked them. These two novelists were in full action; and they kept the public busy. Realism was strong in the market; people did not know then, as we do now, that *The Cloister and the Hearth* was worth all the rest of Charles Reade put together. Had *Lorna Doone* appeared toward the end of the century, when the Romantic Revival was in full swing, it would have received a royal welcome. But how many would have recognised its superiority to the tinsel stuff of those recent days, full of galvanised knights and stuffed chatelaines? For *Lorna* belongs to a class of fiction with which we were flooded in the nineties, though, compared with the ordinary representative of its kind, it is as a star to a glow-worm. Readers then enjoyed impossible characters, whose talk was mainly of "gramercy" and similar curiosities, for they had the opportunity to "revel in the glamour of a bogus antiquity." But an abundance of counterfeits does not lower the value of the real metal; and *Lorna* is a genuine coin struck from the mint of historical romance. In the original preface its author modestly said: —

"This work is called a 'romance,' because the incidents, characters, time, and scenery are alike romantic. And in shaping this old tale, the writer neither dares, nor desires, to claim for it the dignity or cumber it with the difficulty of an historic novel."

In warmth and colour, in correct visualisation, and in successful imitation of the prose of a bygone day (which no one has ever perfectly accomplished), it ranks not very far below the greatest of all English historical romances, *Henry Esmond*.

Lorna Doone is practically one more illustration

of Single-Speech Hamilton. After its appearance, its author wrote and published steadily for thirty years; but the fact remains that not only is *Lorna* his best-known work, but that his entire reputation hangs upon it. Many of his other stories are good, notably *Cripps the Carrier* and *Perlycross;* the latter has a most ingenious plot; but these two now peacefully repose with their mates in undisturbed slumber at dusty library corners. They had an initial sale because they came from the hand that created *Lorna;* then they were lost in the welter of ephemeral literature. Mr. Blackmore offered his buyers all sorts of wares, but, after a momentary examination, they declined what was "just as good," and returned to their favourite, which, by the way, was never his; he ranked it third among his productions.

For this novel is not only one of the best-loved books in English fiction, and stands magnificently the severe test of rereading, it is bound to have even more admirers in the future than it has ever yet enjoyed; it is visibly growing in reputation every year. It may be interesting to analyse some of its elements, in order to understand what has given it so assured a place. The main plot is simplicity itself. It is a history, however, that the world has always found entertaining, the history of the love of a strong man for a beautiful girl. They meet, he falls in love, he rescues her from peril, she goes up to London, becomes a great lady, returns, is dangerously wounded on her wedding-day, recovers, and they live happily for ever after — *voilà tout.* A very simple plot, yet the telling fills two stout volumes, with the reader's interest maintained from first to last.

It is told in the first person — the approved method of the historical romance. Professor Raleigh has admirably pointed out the virtues and defects of the three ways of composing a novel, — direct discourse by the chief actor, the exclusive employment of letters, and the "invisible and omniscient" impersonal author.[1] It is interesting to note, in passing, that our first English novelist, Defoe, adopted the first method; Richardson, our second novelist, took the second; and Fielding, our third novelist, took the third. Now, the great advantage of having John Ridd speak throughout is the gain in reality and vividness; it is as though we sat with him in the ingle, and obtained all our information at first hand. What is lost by narrowness of experience is made up in intensity; we follow him breathlessly, as Desdemona followed Othello, and he has every moment our burning sympathy. We participate more fully in his joys and sorrows, in the agony of his suspense; we share his final triumph. He is talking directly to

[1] *The English Novel*, Chapter VI.

236

us, and John Ridd is a good talker. He is the kind
of man who appeals to all classes of listeners. He
has the gentleness and modesty that are so becoming
to great physical strength; the love of children,
animals, and all helpless creatures; reverence for
God, purity of heart, and a noble slowness to wrath.
Such a man is simply irresistible, and we are sorry
when he finishes his tale. The defect in this method
of narration, which Mr. Blackmore has employed
with such success, is the inevitable defect in all
stories written in this manner, as Professor Raleigh
has observed: "It takes from the novelist the privilege of killing his hero." When John Ridd is
securely bound, and the guns of hostile soldiers are
levelled at his huge bulk, with their fingers actually
on the triggers, we laugh at ourselves for our high-
beating hearts; for of course he is unkillable, else
how could he be talking at this very moment?

The plot of *Lorna Doone*, which, as we have observed, is very simple, is, nevertheless, skilfully
complicated. It is not a surprise plot, like that of
A Pair of Blue Eyes; we are not stunned by the
last page. It is a suspense plot; we have a well-
founded hope that all will come right in the end,
and yet the author has introduced enough disturb-
ing elements to put us occasionally in a maze. This
artistic suspense is attained partly by the method
of direct discourse; which, at the same time, develops

the character of the hero. Big John repeats incidents, dwells lengthily on minute particulars,
stops to enjoy the scenery, and makes mountains of
stories out of molehills of fact. The second com-
plication of the plot arises from the introduction of
characters that apparently divert the course of the
story without really doing so. There are nineteen
important characters, all held well in hand; and a
conspicuous example of a complicating personage is
little Ruth Huckaback. She interferes in the main
plot in an exceedingly clever way. The absorbing
question in every reader's mind is, of course, Will
John marry Lorna? Now Ruth's interviews with
the hero are so skilfully managed, and with such
intervals of time between, that on some pages she
seems destined to be his bride. And, admirably
drawn as her character is, when her artistic purpose
in the plot is fully accomplished, she quietly fades
out, with the significant tribute, "Ruth Huckaback
is not married yet."

There is also a subsidiary plot, dovetailed neatly
into the main building. This is the story of the
attractive highwayman, Tom Faggus, and his love
for John's sister, Annie. Many pages are taken
up with the adventures of this gentleman, who enters
the novel on horseback (what a horse!) at the moment when the old drake is fighting for his life.
Besides our interest in Tom himself, in his wild

adventures, and in his reformation, we are interested in the conflict of his two passions, one for the
bottle, and one for Annie, and we wonder which will
win. This subsidiary love story is still further complicated by the introduction of young De Whiche-
halse; and in the struggle between John Ridd and
the Doones, both Tom Faggus and the De Whiche-
halse family play important parts. It is interesting,
too, to observe how events that seem at the time to
be of no particular importance, turn out later to
be highly significant; when, at the very beginning
of the long story, the little boy, on his way home
from school, meets the lady's maid, and shortly
after sees the child borne away on the robber's
saddle, we imagine all this is put in to enliven the
journey, that it is just "detail"; long afterwards
we find the artistic motive. In fact, one of the most
notable virtues of this admirable plot is the constant
introduction of matters apparently irrelevant and
due to mere garrulity, such as the uncanny sound,
for example, which prove after all to be essential
to the course of the narrative.

As for the characters, they impress us differently
in different moods. For all John Ridd's prodigious
strength, marvellous escapes, and astounding feats,
his personality is so intensely human that he seems
real. His *soul*, at any rate, is genuine, and wholly
natural; his bodily activity — the extraction of

Carver's biceps, the wrenching of the branch from the tree, the hurling of the cannon through the door — makes him a dim giant in a fairy story. When we think of the qualities of his mind and heart, he comes quite close; when we think of his physical prowess, he almost vanishes in the land of Fable. I remember the comment of an undergraduate — "John Ridd is as remote as Achilles; he is like a Greek myth."

The women are all well drawn and individualised — except the heroine. I venture to say that no one has ever seen Lorna in his mind's eye. She is like a plate that will not develop. A very pretty girl with an affectionate disposition, — what more can be said? But so long as a Queen has beauty and dignity, she does not need to be interesting; and Lorna is the queen of this romance. John's mother and his two sisters are as like and unlike as members of the same family ought to be; they are real women. Ruth Huckaback and Gwenny Carfax are great additions to our literary acquaintances; each would make an excellent heroine for a realistic novel. They have the indescribable puzzling characteristics that we call feminine; sudden caprices, flashes of unexpected jealousy, deep loyal tenderness, unlimited capacity for self-sacrifice, and in the last analysis, Mystery.

The humour of the story is spontaneous, and of

great variety, running from broad mirth to whimsical subtlety. The first concerted attack on the Doones is comic opera burlesque; but the scenes of humour that delight us most are those describing friendly relations with beast and bird. The eye of the old drake, as he stared wildly from his precarious position, and the delight of the ducks as they welcomed his rescue; above all, Annie's care of the wild birds in the bitter cold.

"There was not a bird but knew her well, after one day of comforting; and some would come to her hand, and sit, and shut one eye, and look at her. Then she used to stroke their heads, and feel their breasts, and talk to them; and not a bird of them all was there but liked to have it done to him. And I do believe they would eat from her hand things unnatural to them, lest she should be grieved and hurt by not knowing what to do for them. One of them was a noble bird, such as I had never seen before, of very fine bright plumage, and larger than a missel-thrush. He was the hardest of all to please; and yet he tried to do his best."

Whatever may be the merits of Mr. Blackmore's published verse, there is more poetry in *Lorna Doone* than in many volumes of formal rime. The wonderful descriptions of the country in shade and shine, in fog and drought, the pictures of the sunrise and the falling water, the "tumultuous privacy" of the snow-storms, — these are all descriptive poems. Every reader has noticed the peculiar rhythm of the style, and wondered if it were intentional.

Hundreds of sentences here and there are perfect English hexameters; one can find them by opening the book at random, and reading aloud. But this peculiar element in the style goes much farther than isolated phrases. There are solid passages of steady rhythm, which might correctly be printed in verse form.[1]

Mr. Blackmore's personal character was so modest, unassuming, and lovable, that it is not difficult to guess the source of the purity, sweetness, and sincerity of his great book. If he were somewhat surprised at the utter coldness of its first reception, he never got over his amazement at the size and extent of its ultimate triumph. In the preface to the sixth edition, he said: —

"Few things have surprised me more, and nothing has more pleased me, than the great success of this simple tale. . . . Therefore any son of Devon may imagine, and will not grudge, the writer's delight at hearing from a recent visitor to the west, that '*Lorna Doone*, to a Devonshire man, is as good as clotted cream, almost!'

"Although not half so good as that, it has entered many a tranquil, happy, pure, and hospitable home; and the author, while deeply grateful for this genial reception, ascribes it partly to the fact that his story contains no word or thought disloyal to its birthright in the fairest county of England."

---

[1] A writer in the *Atlantic Monthly* notes especially the closing paragraph of Chapter XXVIII, and parts of Chapter XXIX.

Mr. Blackmore lived long enough to see an entirely different kind of "local colour" become conventional, where many a novelist, portraying his native town or the community in which he dwelt, emphasised with what skill he could command all its poverty, squalor, and meanness; the disgusting vices and malignant selfishness of its inhabitants; and after he had thus fouled his nest by representing it as a mass of filth, degradation, and sin, he imagined he had created a work of art. The author of *Lorna Doone* had the satisfaction of knowing that he had inspired hundreds of thousands of readers with the love of his favourite west country, and with an intense desire to visit it. And being, like John Ridd, of a forgiving nature, he forgave America for its early neglect of his story; for being informed of the supremacy of *Lorna Doone* in the hearts of American undergraduates, he remarked, in a letter to the present writer, "The good word of the young, who are at once the most intelligent and the most highly educated of a vast intellectual nation, augurs well for the continuance — at least for a generation — of my fortunate production."

APPENDIX A

NOVELS AS A UNIVERSITY STUDY

Some fourteen years ago, in the pamphlet of elective courses of study open to the senior and junior classes of Yale College, I announced a new course called "Modern Novels." The course and its teacher immediately became the object of newspaper notoriety, which spells academic damnation. From every State in the Union long newspaper clippings were sent to me, in which my harmless little pedagogical scheme was discussed — often under enormous headlines — as a revolutionary idea. It was praised by some, denounced by others, but thoroughly advertised, so that, for many months, I received letters from all parts of the Western Hemisphere, asking for the list of novels read and the method pursued in studying them. During six months these letters averaged three a day, and they came from the north, south, east, and west, from Alaska, Hawaii, Central and South America. The dust raised by all this hubbub crossed the Atlantic. The course was gravely condemned in a column editorial in the London *Daily Telegraph,* and finally received the crowning honour of a parody in *Punch.*

Things have changed somewhat in the last ten years, and although I have never repeated my one year's experiment, I believe that it would be perfectly safe to do so. Not only does the production of new novels continue at constantly accelerating speed, but critical books on the novel have begun to increase and multiply in all directions. At least twenty such works now stand on my shelves, the latest of which (by Selden L. Whitcomb) is frankly called "The Study of a Novel," and boldly begins: "This volume is the result of practical experience in teaching the novel, and its aim is primarily pedagogical."

The objections usually formulated against novels as a university study are about as follows: (*a*) the study of fiction is unacademic — that is, lacking in dignity; (*b*) students will read too many novels anyway, and the emphasis should therefore be thrown on other forms of literary art; (*c*) most recent and contemporary fiction is worthless, and if novels are to be taught at all, the titles selected should be confined entirely to recognised classics; (*d*) many of the novels of to-day are immoral, and the reading of them will corrupt rather than develop adolescent minds; (*e*) they are too "easy," too interesting, and a course confined to them is totally lacking in mental discipline. These objections, each and all, contain some truth, and demand a serious answer.

That the study of fiction is unacademic is a weighty argument, but its weight is the mass of custom and prejudice rather than solid thought. In old times, the curriculum had little to do with real life, so that the most scholarly professors and the most promising pupils were often plentifully lacking in common sense. Students gifted with real independence of mind, marked with an alert interest in the life and thought about them, chafed irritably under the old-fashioned course of study, and often treated it with neglect or open rebellion. What Thomas Gray said of the Cambridge curriculum constitutes a true indictment against eighteenth-century universities; and it was not until very recent times that such studies as history, European literature, modern languages, political economy, natural sciences, and the fine arts were thought to have equal academic dignity with the trinity of Latin, Greek, and mathematics. There are, indeed, many able and conscientious men who still believe that this trinity cannot be successfully rivalled by any other possible group of studies. Now the novel is the most prominent form of modern literary art; and if modern literature is to be studied at all, fiction cannot be overlooked. The profound change brought about in university curricula, caused largely by the elective system, is simply the bringing of college courses of study into closer contact with human life, and the recognition that what young men need is a general preparation to live a life of active usefulness in modern social relations.

That students read too many novels anyway — that is, in proportion to their reading in history and biography — is probably true. But the primary object of a course in novel-reading is not to make the student read more novels, instead of less, nor to substitute the reading of fiction for the reading of other books. The real object is (after a cheerful recognition of the fact that he will read novels anyway) to persuade him to read them intelligently, to observe the difference between good novels and bad, and so to become impatient and disgusted with cheap, sensational, and counterfeit specimens of the novelist's art.

> "The common problem, yours, mine, everyone's,
> Is — not to fancy what were fair in life
> Provided it could be — but, finding first
> What may be, then find how to make it fair
> Up to our means: a very different thing!
> No abstract intellectual plan of life
> Quite irrespective of life's plainest laws,
> But one, a man, who is man and nothing more,
> May lead within a world which (by your leave)
> Is Rome or London, not Fool's Paradise."

That much of contemporary fiction is worthless, and that the novels selected should be classics, is a twofold statement, of which the first phrase is true and the second a *non sequitur*. Much ancient and mediæval literature read in college is worthless in itself; it is read because it illustrates the language, or represents some literary form, or because it throws light on the customs and ideas of the time. The fact that a certain obscure work was written in the year 1200 does not necessarily prove that it is more valuable for study than one written in 1909. Now it so happens that the modern novel has become more and more the mirror of modern ideas; and for a student who really wishes to know what people are thinking about all over the world to-day, the novels of Tolstoi, Björnson, Sudermann, and Thomas Hardy cannot wisely be neglected. Why should the study of the contemporary novel and the contemporary drama be tabooed when in other departments of research the aim is to be as contemporary as possible? We have courses in social conditions that actually investigate slums. I am not for a moment pleading that the study of modern novels and modern art should supplant the study of immortal masterpieces; but merely that they should have their rightful place, and not be regarded either with contempt or as unworthy of serious treatment. The two most beneficial ways to study a novel are to regard it, first, as an art-form, and secondly as a manifestation of intellectual life; from neither point of view should the contemporary novel be wholly neglected.

That many of the novels of to-day are immoral is true, but it is still more true of the classics. The proportion of really immoral books to the total production is probably less to-day than it ever was before; in fact, there are an immense number of excellent contemporary novels which are spotless, something that cannot be said of the classics of antiquity or of the great majority of literary works published prior to the nineteenth century. If immorality be the cry, what shall we say about Aristophanes or Ovid? How does the case stand with the comedies of Dryden or with the novels of Henry Fielding? No, it is undoubtedly true that the teacher who handles modern fiction can more easily find a combination of literary excellence and purity of tone than he could in any previous age.

That a course in novels lacks mental discipline and is too easy depends mainly on the teacher and his method. As regards the time consumed in preparation, it is probable that a student would expend three or four times the number of hours on a course in novels than he would in ancient languages, where, unfortunately, the use of a translation is all but universal; and the translation is fatal to mental discipline. But it is not merely a matter of hours; novels can be taught in such a way as to produce the best kind of mental discipline, which consists, first, in compelling a student to do his own thinking, and, secondly, to train him properly in the expression of what ideas he has.

APPENDIX B

THE TEACHER'S ATTITUDE TOWARD CONTEMPORARY LITERATURE

Two things must be admitted at the start — first, that no person is qualified to judge the value of new books who is not well acquainted with the old ones; second, that the only test of the real greatness of any book is Time. It is, of course, vain to hope that any remarks made on contemporary authors will not be misrepresented, but I have placed two axioms at the beginning of this article in order to clear the ground. I am not advocating the abandonment of the study of Homer and Vergil, or proposing to substitute in their stead the study of Hall Caine, Mrs. Ward, and Marie Corelli. I do not believe that Mr. Pinero is a greater dramatist than Sophokles, or that the mental discipline gained by reading *The Jungle* is equivalent to that obtained in the mastery of Euclid.

I am merely pleading that every thoughtful man who is alive in this year of grace should not attempt to live his whole life in the year 400 B.C., even though he be so humble an individual as a teacher. The very word "teacher" means something more than "scholar"; and scholarship means something more than the knowledge of things that are dead. A good teacher will remember that the boys and girls who come under his instruction are not all going to spend their lives in the pursuit of technical learning. It is his business to influence them; and he cannot exert a powerful influence without some interest in the life and thought of his own day, in the environment in which his pupils exist. I believe that the cardinal error of a divinity-school education is that the candidate for the ministry spends over half his time and energy in the laborious study of Hebrew, whereas he should study the subjects that primarily interest not his colleagues, but his audience.

> "Priests
> Should study passion; how else cure mankind,
> Who come for help in passionate extremes?"

A preacher who knows Hebrew, Greek, systematic theology, New Testament interpretation, and who knows nothing about literature, history, art, and human nature, is grotesquely unfitted for his noble profession.

In every age it has been the fashion to ridicule and decry the literary production of that particular time. I suppose that the greatest creative period that the world has ever known occurred in England during the years 1590–1616, and here is what Ben Jonson said in 1607: "Now, especially in dramatic, or, as they term it, stage-poetry, nothing but ribaldry, profanation, blasphemy, all license of offence to God and man is practised. I dare not deny a great part of this, and am sorry I dare not." In 1610 he wrote, "Thou wert never more fair in the way to be cozened, than in this age, in poetry, especially in plays; wherein, now the concupiscence of dances and of antics so reigneth, as to run away from nature and be afraid of her, is the only point of art that tickles the spectators." And in 1611 he said, "In so thick and dark an ignorance as now almost covers the age . . . you dare, in these jig-given times, to countenance a legitimate poem." And the age which he damned is now regarded as the world's high-water mark!

A man who teaches physics and chemistry is supposed to be familiar not only with the history of his subject, but its latest manifestations; with the work of his contemporaries. A man who teaches political economy and sociology must read the most recent books on these themes both in Europe and America — nay, he must read the newspapers and study the markets, or he will be outstripped by his own pupils. A man who teaches drawing and painting should not only know the history of art, but its latest developments. And yet, when the teacher of literature devotes a small portion of the time of his pupils to the contemplation of contemporary poets, novelists, and dramatists, he is not only blamed for doing so, but some teachers who are ignorant of the writers of their own day boast of their ignorance with true academic pride.

A teacher cannot read every book that appears; he cannot neglect the study and teaching of the recognised classics; but his attitude toward the writers of his own time should not be one of either indifference or contempt. The teacher of English literature should not be the last man in the world to discover the name of an author whom all the world is talking about. And I believe that every great university should offer, under proper restrictions, at least one course in the contemporary drama, or in contemporary fiction, or in some form of contemporary literary art. The Germans are generally regarded as the best scholars in the world, and they never think it beneath their dignity to recognise living authors of distinction. While the British public were condemning in true British fashion an author whom they had not read — Henrik Ibsen — German universities were offering courses exclusively devoted to the study of his works. Imagine a course in Ibsen at Oxford!

But not only should the teacher take an intelligent interest in contemporary authors who have already won a wide reputation, he should be eternally watchful, eternally hopeful — ready to detect signs of promise in the first books of writers whose names are wholly unknown. This does not mean that he should exaggerate the merits of every fresh work, nor beslobber with praise every ambitious quill-driver. On the contrary, — if there be occasion to give an opinion at all, — he should not hesitate to condemn what seems to him shallow, trivial, or counterfeit, no matter how big a "seller" the object in his vision may be. But his sympathies should be warm and keen, and his mind always responsive, when a new planet swims into his ken. One of the most joyful experiences of my life came to me some years ago when I read *Bob, Son of Battle* with the unknown name Alfred Ollivant on the title-page. It was worth wading through tons of trash to find such a jewel.

And is the literature of our generation really slight and mean? By "Contemporary Literature" we include perhaps authors who have written or who are writing during the lifetime of those who are now, let us say, thirty years old. Contemporary literature would then embrace, in the drama, Ibsen, Björnson, Victor Hugo, Henri Becque, Rostand, Maeterlinck, Sudermann, Hauptmann, Pinero, Jones, and others; in the novel, Turgenev, Tolstoi, Dostoievsky, Björnson, Hugo, Daudet, Zola, Maupassant, Heyse, Sudermann, Hardy, Meredith, Stevenson, Kipling,

APPENDIX B

Howells, Mark Twain, and many others; in poetry,
to speak of English writers alone, Tennyson, Browning, Arnold, Swinburne, Morris, Kipling, Phillips,
Watson, Thompson, and others. Those who live
one hundred years from now will know more about
the permanent value of the works of these men than
we do; but are these names really of no importance
to teachers whose speciality is literature?

APPENDIX C

TWO POEMS

It is interesting to compare the two following poems, written by two distinguished English novelists, both men of fine intelligence, noble character, and absolute sincerity. Mr. Hardy's poem appeared in the *Fortnightly Review*, for 1 January, 1907.

NEW YEAR'S EVE

By Thomas Hardy

"I have finished another year," said God,
  "In grey, green, white, and brown;
I have strewn the leaf upon the sod,
Sealed up the worm within the clod,
  And let the last sun down."

"And what's the good of it?" I said,
  "What reasons made You call
From formless void this earth I tread,
When nine-and-ninety can be read
  Why nought should be at all?

"Yea, Sire; why shaped You us, 'who in
  This tabernacle groan'? —
If ever a joy be found herein,
Such joy no man had wished to win
  If he had never known!"

Then He: "My labours logicless
  You may explain; not I:

Sense-sealed I have wrought, without a guess
That I evolved a Consciousness
    To ask for reasons why!

"Strange, that ephemeral creatures who
    By my own ordering are,
Should see the shortness of my view,
Use ethic tests I never knew,
    Or made provision for!"

He sank to raptness as of yore,
    And opening New Year's Day
Wove it by rote as theretofore,
And went on working evermore
    In his unweeting way.

DOMINUS ILLUMINATIO MEA

By Richard Doddridge Blackmore

I

In the hour of death, after this life's whim,
When the heart beats low, and the eyes grow dim,
And pain has exhausted every limb —
    The lover of the Lord shall trust in Him.

2

When the will has forgotten the life-long aim,
And the mind can only disgrace its fame,
And a man is uncertain of his own name,
    The power of the Lord shall fill this frame.

3

When the last sigh is heaved and the last tear shed,
And the coffin is waiting beside the bed,
And the widow and the child forsake the dead,
    The angel of the Lord shall lift this head.

4

For even the purest delight may pall,
The power must fail, and the pride must fall,
And the love of the dearest friends grow small —
    But the glory of the Lord is all in all.

This poem, with the signature "R. D. B. in memoriam M. F. G." first appeared in the *University Magazine* in 1879. Although it has been included in some anthologies, the author's name was kept an absolute secret until July, 1909. In the *Athenæum* for 3 July, 1909, was printed an interesting letter from Agnes E. Cook, by which we learn that the late Mr. Blackmore actually *dreamed* this poem, in its exact language and metre. The letter from the author which was published in the same *Athenæum* article, gives the facts connected with this extraordinary dream.

Tedd^n Jany 5th 1879.

My Dear Sir.

Having lately been at the funeral of a most dear relation I was there again (in a dream) last night, and heard the mourners sing the lines enclosed, which impressed me so that I was able to write them without change of a word this morning. I never heard or read them before to my knowledge. They do not look so well on paper as they sounded; but if you like to print them, here they are. Only please not to put my name beyond initials or send me money for them. With all good wishes to Mrs. Cook and yourself

Very truly yours

R. D. Blackmore.

K Cook Esqre L.L.D.

LIST OF PUBLICATIONS

By Andrew Keogh

[The twelve authors are in alphabetical order. The books of each are in chronological order, the assigned dates being those of the publishers' trade journals in which the fact of publication was first recorded. Novels originally issued as serials have a note giving the name and date of the original magazine.]

BJÖRNSTJERNE BJÖRNSON

8 December 1832–
[Including only works that have been translated into English.]

1857, Sept. 1.   Synnöve Solbakken. Christiania. (*Illustreret Folkeblad*, 1857.)
— Trust and Trial. [A translation by Mary Howitt.] London, Hurst, Sept. 15, 1858.
— Love and Life in Norway. Tr. by the Hon. Augusta Bethell and A. Plesner. London, Cassell [1870].
— Synnöve Solbakken. Tr. by R. B. Anderson. Boston, Houghton, 1881.
— Synnöve Solbakken. Given in English by Julie Sutter. London, Macmillan, 1881.

1858.   Arne. Bergen, 1858 [1859].
— Arne; or, Peasant Life in Norway. Tr. by a Norwegian. Bergen [1861].
— Arne: a Sketch of Norwegian Country

Life. Tr. by A. Plesner and S. Rugely.
Powers. London, Strahan, Aug. 1,
1866.

— Arne. Tr. by R. B. Anderson. Boston,
Houghton, 1881.

— Arne, and the Fisher Lassie. Tr. with an
introd. by W. Low. London, Bell, 1890.

1860. En glad Gut. Christiania. (*Aftenbladet.*)

— Ovind. Tr. by S. and E. Hjerleid. London, 1869.

— The Happy Boy. Tr. by Helen R. Gade.
Boston, Sever, 1870.

— A Happy Boy. Tr. by R. B. Anderson.
Boston, Houghton, 1881.

— The Happy Lad, and other Tales. London, Blackie, 1882.

1862. Sigurd Slembe. Copenhagen.

— Sigurd Slembe: a Dramatic Trilogy. Tr.
by W. M. Payne. Boston, Houghton,
Oct. 20, 1888.

1865. De Nygifte. Copenhagen.

— The Newly Married Couple. Tr. by S.
and E. Hjerleid. London, Simpkin,
1870.

1868, Apr. Fiskerjenten. Copenhagen.

— The Fisher-Maiden: a Norwegian Tale.
From the author's German edition by
M. E. Niles. N.Y., Holt, 1869.

— The Fishing Girl. Tr. by A. Plesner and
F. Richardson. London, Cassell [1870].

— The Fisher Girl. Tr. by S. and E.
Hjerleid. London, Simpkin, 1871
[1870].

— The Fisher Maiden. Tr. by R. B.
Anderson. Boston, Houghton, 1882.

	— Arne and the Fisher Lassie. Tr. with an introd. by W. Low. London, Bell, 1890.
1873.	Brude–Slaatten: Fortælling. Copenhagen.
	— Life by the Fells and Fiords. A Norwegian Sketch-book [containing a translation of the Bridal March]. London, Strahan, 1879.
	— The Bridal March and other Stories. Tr. by R. B. Anderson. Boston, 1882.
	— The Wedding March. Tr. by M. Ford. N.Y., Munro, 1882.
1877, Oct.	Magnhild: en Fortælling. Copenhagen.
	— Magnhild. Tr. by R. B. Anderson. Boston, Houghton, 1883 [1882].
1879, Aug.	Kaptejn Mansana. Copenhagen.
	— Captain Mansana, and other Stories. Tr. by R. B. Anderson. Cambridge, Mass., 1882.
	— Captain Mansana. N.Y., Munro, 1882.
	— Captain Mansana, and Mother's Hands. N.Y., Macmillan, 1897.
1883, Sept.	En Hanske: Skuespil. Copenhagen.
	— A Glove: a Prose Play. (*Poet-Lore*, Jan.-July, 1892.)
	— A Gauntlet. Tr. by H. L. Braekstad. London, French [1890].
	— A Gauntlet. Tr. by Osman Edwards. London, Longmans, 1894.
Nov.	Over Ævne. Første Stykke. Copenhagen.
	— Pastor Sang: being the Norwegian drama Over Ævne [Part 1]. Tr. by W. Wilson. London, Longmans, 1893.
1884, Oct.	Det flager i Byen og på Havnen. Copenhagen.

	— The Heritage of the Kurts. Tr. by C. Fairfax. London, Heinemann, 1892.
1887, Aug.	Støv. (Originally published in 1882 in I. Hfte *Nyt Tidsskrift*.)
	— Magnhild and Dust. N.Y., Macmillan, 1897.
1889, Oct.	På Guds Veje. Copenhagen.
	— In God's Way. N.Y., Lovell, 1889.
	— In God's way: a Novel. Tr. by E. Carmichael. London, Heinemann, 1890.
1895, Dec.	Over Ævne. Andet Stykke. Copenhagen.
1898, Nov.	Paul Lange og Tora Parsberg. Copenhagen.
	— Tr. by H. L. Braekstad. London, N.Y., Harper, Feb., 1899.
1901, Apr.	Laboremus. Copenhagen.
	— Laboremus. London, Chapman, June 8, 1901. (First published as literary supplement to the *Fortnightly Review*, May, 1901.)
1906, Oct.	Mary: Fortælling. Copenhagen.
	— Mary. Tr. by Mary Morison. N.Y., Macmillan, Sept. 4, 1909.

In addition to the works listed above, most of the tales and sketches in Björnson's three collections (Smaastykker, Bergen, 1860; Fortællinger, Copenhagen, 1872; Nye Fortællinger, Copenhagen, 1894) have appeared in English in one or other of the collections listed below: —

Life by the Fells and Fiords: a Norwegian Sketch-book. London, Strahan [1879]. *Contents:* Arne. — The Bridal March. — The Churchyard and the Railroad. — The Father. — Faithfulness. — Thrond. — Blakken. — A Life's Enigma. — Checked Imagination. — The Eagle's

Nest. — A Dangerous Wooing. — The Brothers' Quarrel. — The Eagle and the Fir. — Poems.

Works. American edition, translated by R. B. Anderson. 3 v. Boston, Houghton, 1884. *Contents:* v. 1. Synnöve Solbakken. — Arne. — Early Tales and Sketches: The Railroad and the Churchyard. — Thrond. — A Dangerous Wooing. — The Bear-Hunter. — The Eagle's Nest. — v. 2. A Happy Boy. — The Fisher Maiden. — Tales and Sketches: Blakken. — Fidelity. — A Problem of Life. — v. 3. The Bridal March. — Captain Mansana. — Magnhild. — Dust.

Novels. Edited by Edmund Gosse. London, Heinemann; N.Y., Macmillan. 13 v. 1894–1909. *Contents:* v. 1. Synnöve Solbakken. Given in English by Julie Sutter. A new ed. . . . 1895. — v. 2. Arne. Tr. by W. Low. 1895. — v. 3. A Happy Boy. Tr. by Mrs. W. Archer. 1896. — v. 4. The Fisher Lass. 1896. — v. 5. The Bridal March, and One Day. 1896. — v. 6. Magnhild and Dust. 1897. — v. 7. Captain Mansana, and Mother's Hands. 1897. — v. 8. Absalom's Hair, and A Painful Memory. 1898. — v. 9–10. In God's Way. Tr. by E. Carmichael. 1908. — v. 11–12. The Heritage of the Kurts. Tr. by Cecil Fairfax. 1908. — v. 13. Mary. Tr. by Mary Morison. 1909.

RICHARD DODDRIDGE BLACKMORE
7 June 1825–20 January 1900

1854, May 1.	Poems by Melanter. London, Saunders.
July.	Epullia, and other Poems. By the Author of Poems by Melanter. London, Hope.
1855, Jan. 16.	The Bugle of the Black Sea; or, The British in the East. By Melanter. London, Hardwicke.
1860, Oct. 27.	The Fate of Franklin. London, Hardwicke.

1862, July 31.

The Farm and Fruit of Old: a Translation in Verse of the first and second Georgics of Virgil. By a Market Gardener. London, Low.

1864, Mar. 31.

Clara Vaughan: a Novel. 3 vols. London, Macmillan.

1866, Sept. 1.

Cradock Nowell: A Tale of the New Forest. 3 vols. London, Chapman. (*Macmillan's Magazine*, May, 1865–Aug., 1866.)

1869, Apr. 1.

Lorna Doone: a Romance of Exmoor. 3 vols. London, Low.

1871, Apr. 1.

The Georgics of Virgil, translated. London, Low.

1872, Aug. 2.

The Maid of Sker. 3 vols. London, Blackwood. (*Blackwood's Magazine*, Aug., 1871–July, 1872.)

1875, May 1.

Alice Lorraine: a Tale of the South Downs. 3 vols. London, Low. (*Blackwood's Magazine*, Mar., 1874–Apr., 1875.)

1876, June 1.

Cripps the Carrier: a Woodland Tale. 3 vols. London, Low.

1877, Nov. 16.

Erema; or, My Father's Sin. 3 vols. London, Smith, Elder. (*Cornhill Magazine*, Nov., 1876–Nov., 1877.)

1880, May 15.

Mary Anerley: a Yorkshire Tale. 3 vols. London, Low. (*Fraser's Magazine*, July, 1879–Sept., 1880.)

1881, Dec. 31.

Christowell: a Dartmoor Tale. 3 vols. London, Low. (*Good Words*, Jan.–Dec., 1881.)

1884, May 15.

The Remarkable History of Sir Thomas Upmore. 2 vols. London, Low.

1887, Mar. 1.

Springhaven: a Tale of the Great War.

	3 vols. London, Low. (*Harper's Magazine*, Apr., 1886–Apr., 1887.)
1889, Dec. 31.	Kit and Kitty: a Story of West Middlesex. 3 vols. London, Low, 1890 [1889].
1894, Aug. 25.	Perlycross: a Tale of the Western Hills. 3 vols. London, Low.
1895, June 22.	Fringilla: Some Tales in Verse. London, Mathews.
1896, Mar. 21.	Tales from the Telling-House. London, Low.
1897, Nov. 27.	Dariel: a Romance of Surrey. London, Blackwood.

SAMUEL LANGHORNE CLEMENS
30 November 1835–

1867, May 1.	The Celebrated Jumping Frog of Calaveras County, and other Sketches. Edited by John Paul. N.Y., Amer. News Co.
1869, Oct. 1.	The Innocents Abroad; or, The New Pilgrim's Progress. Hartford, American Publ. Co.
1871.	Mark Twain's Autobiography and First Romance. N.Y., Sheldon.
1872, Feb. 29.	Roughing it. Hartford, American Publ. Co.
1874, Jan. 3.	The Gilded Age: a Tale of To-Day. By Mark Twain and Charles Dudley Warner. Hartford, American Publ. Co.
	Mark Twain's Sketches. [No. 1.] N.Y., American News Co.
1875.	Mark Twain's Sketches, new and old. Now first published in complete form. Hartford, American Publ. Co.
1876, Dec. 23.	The Adventures of Tom Sawyer. Hartford, American Publ. Co.

1877, Sept. 22.   A True Story, and The Recent Carnival of Crime. Boston, Osgood.

1878, Mar. 23.   Punch, Brothers, Punch! and other Sketches. N.Y., Slote.

1880, July 10.   A Tramp Abroad. Hartford, American Publ. Co.

1882, Jan. 21.   The Prince and the Pauper. Boston, Osgood.

June 17.   The Stolen White Elephant, etc. Boston, Osgood.

1883, July 7.   Life on the Mississippi. Boston, Osgood.

1884, Dec. 31.   The Adventures of Huckleberry Finn, Tom Sawyer's Comrade. London, Chatto. (N.Y., Webster, Mar. 14, 1885.)

1889, Dec. 28.   A Connecticut Yankee in King Arthur's Court: a Satire. N.Y., Webster.

1892, Apr. 9.   Merry Tales. N.Y., Webster.

1893, Apr. 29.   The £1,000,000 Bank-note, and other new stories. N.Y., Webster.

1894, Mar. 2.   The Tragedy of Pudd'nhead Wilson, and the comedy Those Extraordinary Twins. Hartford, American Publ. Co.

Apr. 15.   Tom Sawyer Abroad, by Huck Finn. Edited by Mark Twain. N.Y., Webster.

1896, May 9.   Personal Recollections of Joan of Arc. By the Sieur Louis de Conte (her page and secretary). Freely translated out of the ancient French into modern English from the original unpublished manuscript in the National Archives of France, by Jean François Alden. N.Y., Harper.

1897, Apr. 3.   The American Claimant, and other Stories and Sketches. N.Y., Harper.

Apr. 17.   How to tell a story, and other Essays. N.Y., Harper.

1897, Dec. 11.   Following the Equator: a Journey around the World. Hartford, American Publ. Co. (London, Chatto, under title "More Tramps Abroad.")

1900, June 23.   The Man that Corrupted Hadleyburg, and other Stories and Essays. N.Y., Harper.

1902, Apr. 19.   A Double-barrelled Detective Story. N.Y., Harper.

1904, Apr. 16.   Extracts from Adam's Diary, translated from the Original Manuscript. N.Y., Harper.

Oct. 1.   A Dog's Tale. N.Y., Harper.

1905, Oct. 7.   Editorial Wild Oats. N.Y., Harper.

Nov. 4.   King Leopold's Soliloquy: a Defence of his Congo Rule. Boston, Warren.

1906, June 16.   Eve's Diary, translated from the Original Manuscript. N.Y., Harper.

Oct. 13.   The $30,000 Bequest, and other Stories. N.Y., Harper.

1907, Feb. 16.   Christian Science, with notes containing corrections to date. N.Y., Harper.

Nov. 9.   A Horse's Tale. N.Y., Harper.

1909, Apr. 17.   Is Shakespeare dead? From my Autobiography. N.Y., Harper.

Oct. 23.   Extract from Captain Stormfield's Visit to Heaven. N.Y., Harper.

WILLIAM DE MORGAN
16 November 1839–

1906, July 28.   Joseph Vance: an ill-written Autobiography. London, Heinemann. (N.Y., Holt, Sept. 22.)

1907, June 15.   Alice-for-Short: a Dichronism. N.Y., Holt. (London, Heinemann, June 29.)

| 1908, Feb. 8. | Somehow Good. N.Y., Holt. (London, Heinemann, Feb. 15.) |
| 1909, Nov. 16. | It Never Can Happen Again. N.Y., Holt. (London, Heinemann, 2 v.) |

THOMAS HARDY
2 June 1840–

1871, Apr. 1.	Desperate Remedies: a Novel. 3 vols. London, Tinsley.
1872, Dec. 9.	Under the Greenwood Tree: a Rural Painting of the Dutch School. 2 vols. London, Tinsley.
1873, June 2.	A Pair of Blue Eyes: a Novel. 3 vols. London, Tinsley. (*Tinsley's Magazine*, Sept., 1872–July, 1873.)
1874, Dec. 8.	Far from the Madding Crowd. 2 vols. London, Smith, Elder. (*Cornhill Magazine*, Jan.–Dec., 1874.)
1876, Apr. 15.	The Hand of Ethelberta: a Comedy in Chapters. 2 vols. London, Smith, Elder. (*Cornhill Magazine*, July, 1875–May, 1876.)
1878, Nov. 16.	The Return of the Native. 3 vols. London, Smith, Elder. (Belgravia, Jan.–Dec., 1878.)
1880, Nov. 1.	The Trumpet-Major: a Tale. 3 vols. London, Smith, Elder. (*Good Words*, Jan.–Dec., 1880.)
1881, Dec. 31.	A Laodicean; or, The Castle of the De Stancys: a Story of To-day. 3 vols, London, Low. (*Harper's Magazine*, Jan., 1881–Jan., 1882.)
1882, Nov. 1.	Two on a Tower: a Romance. 3 vols. London, Low. (*Atlantic Monthly*, May–Dec., 1882.)

LIST OF PUBLICATIONS

1884, Jan. 25.	The Romantic Adventures of a Milkmaid: a Novel. N.Y., Munro. (*Graphic*, Summer No. for 1883.)
1886, June 1.	The Mayor of Casterbridge: the Life and Death of a Man of Character. 2 vols. London, Smith, Elder. (*Graphic*, Jan. 2–May 15, 1886.)
1887, Apr. 1.	The Woodlanders. 3 vols. London, Macmillan. (*Macmillan's Magazine*, May, 1886–April, 1887.)
1888, May 15.	Wessex Tales, Strange, Lively, and Commonplace. 2 vols. London, Macmillan.
1891, June 6.	A Group of Noble Dames. London, Osgood. (*Graphic*, Christmas No., 1890.)
Dec. 12.	Tess of the D'Urbervilles: a Pure Woman faithfully presented. 3 vols. London, Osgood, 1892 [1891]. (*Graphic*, July 4–Dec. 26, 1891.)
1894, Feb. 24.	Life's Little Ironies: a Set of Tales. London, Osgood.
1895, Nov. 9.	Jude the Obscure. London, Osgood. (*Harper's Magazine*, Dec., 1894–Nov., 1895. Began as "The Simpletons"; then changed its title to "Hearts Insurgent.")
1897, Mar. 20.	The Well-Beloved: A Sketch of a Temperament. London, Osgood. (The Pursuit of the Well-Beloved, *Illustrated London News*, Oct.–Dec. 1892.)
1898, Dec. 24.	Wessex Poems, and Other Verses. London, Harper.
1901, Nov. 30.	Poems of the Past and the Present. London, Harper.

1904, Jan. 23.	The Dynasts: a Drama of the Napoleonic Wars. Part 1. London, Macmillan.
1906, Feb. 17.	The Dynasts. Part 2. Macmillan.
1908, Feb. 22.	The Dynasts. Part 3. Macmillan.

WILLIAM DEAN HOWELLS
1 March 1837–

1860.	Poems of Two Friends. By John James Piatt and W. D. Howells. Columbus, Follett.
	Lives and Speeches of Abraham Lincoln and Hannibal Hamlin. N.Y., Townsend. [The Biography of Hamlin is by J. L. Hayes.]
1866, Aug. 15.	Venetian Life. N.Y., Hurd.
1867, Dec. 2.	Italian Journeys. N.Y., Hurd.
1868, Dec. 1.	No Love lost: a romance of travel. N.Y. (*Putnam's Magazine*, Dec., 1868.)
1871, Jan. 2.	Suburban Sketches. N.Y., Hurd.
1872, Jan. 1.	Their Wedding Journey. Boston, Osgood. (*Atlantic Monthly*, July–Dec., 1871.)
1873, May 10.	A Chance Acquaintance. Boston, Osgood. (*Atlantic Monthly*, Jan.–June, 1873.)
Sept. 27.	Poems. Boston, Osgood.
1874, Dec. 5.	A Foregone Conclusion. Boston, Osgood, 1875 [1874]. (*Atlantic Monthly*, July–Dec., 1874.)
1876, Feb. 12.	A Day's Pleasure. Boston, Osgood. (*Atlantic Monthly*, July–Sept., 1870.)
Sept. 16.	Sketch of the Life and Character of Rutherford B. Hayes. N.Y., Hurd.
Dec. 9.	The Parlor Car: Farce. Boston, Osgood. (*Atlantic Monthly*, Sept., 1876.)
1877, Apr. 28.	Out of the Question: a Comedy. Boston,

	Osgood. (*Atlantic Monthly*, Feb.–Apr., 1877.)
Oct. 13.	A Counterfeit Presentment: Comedy. Boston, Osgood (*Atlantic Monthly*, Aug.–Oct., 1877.)
1879, Mar. 1.	The Lady of the Aroostook. Boston, Houghton. (*Atlantic Monthly*, Nov., 1878–Mar., 1879.)
1880, June 26.	The Undiscovered Country. Boston, Houghton. (*Atlantic Monthly*, Jan.– July, 1880.)
1881, Aug. 6.	A Fearful Responsibility, and other Stories. Boston, Osgood.
Dec. 10.	Doctor Breen's Practice: a Novel. Boston, Osgood. (*Atlantic Monthly*, Aug.– Dec., 1881.)
1882, Oct. 14.	A Modern Instance: a Novel. Boston, Osgood. (*Century Magazine*, Dec., 1881–Oct., 1882.)
1883, Apr. 28.	The Sleeping-Car: a Farce. Boston, Osgood. (*Harper's Christmas*, Dec., 1882.)
Sept. 29.	A Woman's Reason: a Novel. Boston, Osgood. (*Century*, Feb.–Oct., 1883.)
Dec. 22.	A Little Girl among the Old Masters, with Introduction and Comment by W. D. Howells. Boston, Osgood, 1884 [1883].
1884, Mar. 22.	The Register: Farce. Boston, Osgood. (*Harper's Magazine*, Dec., 1884.)
May 24.	Three Villages. Boston, Osgood.
	Niagara Revisited. Chicago, Dalziel. (Suppressed.) (*Atlantic Monthly*, May, 1883.)
1885, Jan. 31.	The Elevator: Farce. Boston, Osgood. (*Harper's Magazine*, Dec., 1884.)

Aug. 22.	The Rise of Silas Lapham. Boston, Ticknor. (*Century*, Nov., 1884–Aug., 1885.)
Nov. 7.	Tuscan Cities. Boston, Ticknor, 1886 [1885]. (*Century Magazine*, Oct., 1885.)
1886, Jan. 2.	The Garroters: Farce. N.Y., Harper. (*Harper's Magazine*, Dec., 1885.)
Feb. 27.	Indian Summer. Boston, Ticknor. (*Harper's Magazine*, July, 1885–Feb., 1886.)
Dec. 18.	The Minister's Charge; or, The Apprenticeship of Lemuel Barker. Boston, Ticknor, 1887 [1886]. (*Century Magazine*, Feb.–Dec., 1886.)
1887, Oct. 8.	Modern Italian Poets: Essays and Versions. N.Y., Harper.
Dec. 17.	April Hopes. N.Y., Harper, 1888 [1887]. (*Harper's Magazine*, Feb.–Nov., 1887.)
1888, Aug. 11.	A Sea-Change; or, Love's Stowaway: a lyricated Farce. Boston, Ticknor. (*Harper's Weekly*, July 14, 1888.)
Dec. 22.	Annie Kilburn: a Novel. N.Y., Harper, 1889 [1888]. (*Harper's Magazine*, June–Nov., 1888.)
1889, Apr. 20.	The Mouse-Trap, and other Farces. N.Y., Harper. (The Mouse-Trap, *Harper's Magazine*, Dec., 1886.)
Dec. 7.	A Hazard of New Fortunes: a Novel. N.Y., Harper, 1890 [1889]. (*Harper's Weekly*, Mar. 23–Nov. 16, 1889.)
1890, June 7.	The Shadow of a Dream: a Story. N.Y., Harper. (*Harper's Magazine*, Mar.–May, 1890.)
Oct. 18.	A Boy's Town, described for *Harper's Young People*. N.Y., Harper. (*Harper's Young People*, Apr. 8–Aug. 26, 1890.)

1891, May 16.   Criticism and Fiction. N.Y., Harper. [Selections from the "Editor's Study" of *Harper's Magazine*.]

    Oct. 17.   The Albany Depot. N.Y., Harper, 1892 [1891]. (*Harper's Weekly*, Dec. 14, 1889.)

    Dec. 5.   An Imperative Duty: a Novel. N.Y., Harper, 1892 [1891]. (*Harper's Magazine*, July–Oct., 1891.)

1892, Apr. 9.   The Quality of Mercy: a Novel. N.Y., Harper. (*New York (Sunday) Sun*.)

    Aug. 6.   A Letter of Introduction: Farce. N.Y,. Harper. (*Harper's Magazine*, Jan., 1892.)

    Oct. 8.   A Little Swiss Sojourn. N.Y., Harper. (*Harper's Magazine*, Feb.–Mar., 1888.)

    Dec. 17.   Christmas Every Day, and other Stories told for Children. N.Y., Harper, 1893 [1892].

1893, Apr. 1.   The World of Chance: a Novel. N.Y., Harper. (*Harper's Magazine*, Mar.–Nov., 1892.)

    May 20.   The Unexpected Guests: a Farce. N.Y., Harper. (*Harper's Magazine*, Jan., 1893.)

    Oct. 14.   My Year in a Log Cabin. N.Y., Harper. (*Youth's Companion*.)

    Nov. 4.   Evening Dress: Farce. N.Y., Harper. (*Cosmopolitan Magazine*, May, 1892.)

    Nov. 11.   The Coast of Bohemia: a Novel. N.Y., Harper. (*Ladies' Home Journal*, Dec., 1892–Oct., 1893.)

1894, June 2.   A Traveler from Altruria: Romance. N.Y., Harper. (*Cosmopolitan*, Nov, 1892–Oct., 1893.)

1895, June 22.	My Literary Passions. N.Y., Harper. (*Ladies' Home Journal*, Dec., 1892–Oct., 1893.)
Nov. 2.	Stops of Various Quills. N.Y., Harper. (Eleven of the poems appeared in *Harper's Magazine*, Dec., 1894.)
1896, Feb. 22.	The Day of their Wedding: a Novel. N.Y., Harper. (*Harper's Bazar*, Oct. 5–Nov. 16, 1895.)
Apr. 11.	A Parting and a Meeting: Story. N.Y., Harper. (*Cosmopolitan Magazine*, Dec., 1894.)
Oct. 31.	Impressions and Experiences. N.Y., Harper.
1897, Feb. 20.	A Previous Engagement: Comedy. N.Y., Harper. (*Harper's Magazine*, Dec., 1895.)
Apr. 17.	The Landlord at Lion's Head: a Novel. N.Y., Harper. (*Harper's Weekly*, July 4–Dec. 5, 1896.)
Sept. 11.	An Open-Eyed Conspiracy: an Idyl of Saratoga. N.Y., Harper. (*Century Magazine*, July–Oct., 1896.)
Dec. 25.	Stories of Ohio. N.Y., American Book Co.
1898, June 25.	The Story of a Play: a Novel. N.Y., Harper. (*Scribner's Magazine*, Mar.–July, 1897.)
1899, Feb. 25.	Ragged Lady: a Novel. N.Y., Harper.
Dec. 16.	Their Silver Wedding Journey. 2 vols. N.Y., Harper. (*Harper's Magazine*, Jan.–Dec., 1899.)
1900, June 2.	Bride Roses: a Scene. Boston, Houghton.
June 2.	Room Forty-five: a Farce. Boston, Houghton.

Oct. 6.	The Smoking Car: a Farce. Boston, Houghton.
Oct. 6.	An Indian Giver: a Comedy. Boston, Houghton. (*Harper's Magazine*, Jan., 1897.)
Dec. 1.	Literary Friends and Acquaintance: a Personal Retrospect of American Authorship. N.Y., Harper.
1901, June 1.	A Pair of Patient Lovers. N.Y., Harper. (*Harper's Magazine*, Nov., 1897.)
Nov. 2.	Heroines of Fiction. 2 vols. N.Y., Harper. (*Harper's Bazar*, May 5, 1900– Oct., 1901.)
1902, Apr. 26.	The Kentons: a Novel. N.Y., Harper.
Oct. 4.	The Flight of Pony Baker: a Boy's Town Story. N.Y., Harper.
Oct. 25.	Literature and Life: Studies. N.Y., Harper.
1903, June 6.	Questionable Shapes. N.Y., Harper.
Oct. 3.	Letters Home. N.Y., Harper.
1904, Oct. 15.	The Son of Royal Langbrith: a Novel. N.Y., Harper. (*North American Review*, Jan.–Aug., 1904.)
1905, June 17.	Miss Bellard's Inspiration: a Novel. N.Y., Harper.
Oct. 21.	London Films. N.Y., Harper. (*Harper's Magazine*, Dec., 1904–Mar., 1905.)
1906, Nov. 3.	Certain delightful English Towns, with Glimpses of the pleasant country between. N.Y., Harper.
1907, Apr. 27.	Through the Eye of the Needle: a Romance. N.Y., Harper.
June 1.	Mulberries in Pay's Garden. Cincinnati, Clarke.
Nov. 9.	Between the Dark and the Daylight: Romances. N.Y., Harper.

1908, Mar. 21.	Fennel and Rue: a Novel. N.Y., Harper.
Dec. 12.	Roman Holidays, and others. N.Y., Harper.
1909, June 12.	The Mother and the Father: Dramatic Passages. N.Y., Harper. (The Mother, in *Harper's Magazine*, Dec., 1902.)
Nov. 6.	Seven English Cities. N.Y., Harper.

RUDYARD KIPLING
30 December 1865–

1881.	Schoolboy Lyrics. Lahore. (Printed for Private Circulation only.)
1884.	Echoes. By Two Writers. Lahore.
1885.	Quartette. The Christmas Annual of the Civil and Military Gazette. By four Anglo-Indian Writers. Lahore.
1886.	Departmental Ditties. Lahore.
1888.	Plain Tales from the Hills. Calcutta, Thacker.
	Soldiers Three: a Collection of Stories. Allahabad, Wheeler.
	The Story of the Gadsbys: a Tale without a Plot. Allahabad, Wheeler.
	In Black and White. Allahabad, Wheeler.
	Under the Deodars. Allahabad, Wheeler.
	The Phantom 'Rickshaw, and other Tales. Allahabad, Wheeler.
	Wee Willie Winkie, and other Child Stories. Allahabad, Wheeler.
1890, Sept. 6.	The Courting of Dinah Shadd, and other Stories. N.Y., Harper.
	The City of Dreadful Night, and other Sketches. Allahabad, Wheeler.

1891.	The Smith Administration. Allahabad, Wheeler.
	Letters of Marque. Allahabad, Wheeler.
Feb. 28.	The Light that Failed. London, Macmillan. (*Lippincott's Magazine,* Jan., 1891.)
Aug. 15.	Life's Handicap: being stories of mine own people. London, Macmillan.
1892, May 21.	Barrack-Room Ballads, and other Verses. London, Methuen.
July 9.	The Naulahka: a Story of West and East. By Rudyard Kipling and Wolcott Balestier. London, Heinemann. (*Century Magazine,* Nov., 1891–July, 1892.)
1893, June 17.	Many Inventions. London, Macmillan.
1894, June 2.	The Jungle Book. London, Macmillan.
1895.	Good Hunting. Pp. 16. London, *Pall Mall Gazette* office.
Oct. 26.	Out of India: Things I saw, and failed to see, on certain Days and Nights at Jeypore and elsewhere. N.Y., Dillingham.
Nov. 16.	The Second Jungle Book. London, Macmillan.
1896, Nov. 7.	Soldier Tales. London, Macmillan.
Nov. 14.	The Seven Seas. London, Methuen.
1897, Oct. 23.	Captains Courageous: a Story of the Grand Banks. London, Macmillan.
Dec. 4.	An Almanac of Twelve Sports for 1898. By William Nicholson. With accompanying Rhymes by Rudyard Kipling. London, Heinemann.
	White Horses. Pp. 10. London, printed for Private Circulation.
1898, May.	The Destroyers: a new Poem. Pp. 6. London, Ward.

Sept. 10.	Collectanea: being certain reprinted Verses. Pp. 32. N.Y., Mansfield.
Oct. 15.	The Day's Work. London, Macmillan.
Dec. 17.	A Fleet in Being: Notes of two Trips with the Channel Squadron. London, Macmillan.
1899, July 1.	From Sea to Sea: Letters of Travel. 2 vols. N.Y., Doubleday. (London, Macmillan, Feb. 24, 1900.)
Oct. 6.	Stalky and Co. London, Macmillan.
1901, Oct. 19.	Kim. London, Macmillan.
1902, Oct. 11.	Just So Stories for Little Children. London, Macmillan.
1903, Oct. 10.	The Five Nations. London, Methuen.
1904, Oct. 15.	Traffics and Discoveries. London, Macmillan.
1909, Oct. 16.	Actions and Reactions. N.Y., Doubleday.
Oct. 16.	Abaft the Funnel. N.Y., Dodge.
	Cuckoo Song. Pp. 3. N.Y., Doubleday.

ALFRED OLLIVANT
1874–

1898, Oct. 8.	Owd Bob, the Grey Dog of Kenmuir. London, Methuen. (N.Y., Doubleday, Oct. 29, under title "Bob, Son of Battle.")
1902, Nov. 15.	Danny. N.Y., Doubleday. (London, Murray, Feb. 28, 1903, under title "Danny: Story of a Dandie Dinmont.")
1907, Oct. 5.	Redcoat Captain: A Story of That Country. N.Y., Macmillan. (London, Murray, Oct. 19.)
1908, Oct. 17.	The Gentleman: A Romance of the Sea. N.Y., Macmillan. (London, Murray, Oct. 24.)

LIST OF PUBLICATIONS

HENRYK SIENKIEWICZ
4 May 1846–

[Including only works that have been translated into English.]

1884, Nov.   Ogniem i Mieczem. 4 vols. Warsaw.
— With Fire and Sword. Tr. by Jeremiah Curtin. Boston, Little, Brown & Co., May 17, 1890.
— With Fire and Sword. Tr. by Samuel A. Binion. Phila., Altemus.

1886.   Potop. 6 vols. Warsaw.
— The Deluge. Tr. by J. Curtin. 2 vols. Boston, Little, Dec. 19, 1891.

1887–1888.   Pan Wołodyjowski. 3 vols. Warsaw.
— Pan Michael. Tr. by J. Curtin. Boston, Little, Dec. 2, 1893.
— Pan Michael. Tr. by S. A. Binion. Phila., Altemus [1898].

1891, Feb.   Bez Dogmatu. 3 vols. Warsaw.
— Without Dogma. Tr. by Iza Young. Boston, Little, Apr. 15, 1893.

1895, Apr.   Rodzina Połanieckich. 3 vols. Warsaw.
— Children of the Soil. Tr. by J. Curtin. Boston, Little, June 1, 1895.
— The Irony of Life: the Polanetzki Family. Tr. by Nathan M. Babad. N.Y., Fenno, Apr. 28, 1900.

1896, Dec.   Quo Vadis. 3 vols. Warsaw.
— Quo Vadis. Tr. by J. Curtin. Boston, Little, Oct. 17, 1896.
— Quo Vadis. Tr. by S. A. Binion and S. Malevsky. Phila., Altemus, Dec. 18, 1897.
— Quo Vadis. Tr. by Wm. E. Smith. N.Y., Ogilvie, 1898.

1900, Nov.   Krzyżacy. 4 vols. Warsaw.
— Knights of the Cross [Part 1 only]. Tr.
by S. C. de Soissons. N.Y., Fenno, 1897.
— Knights of the Cross. Tr. by J. Curtin.
2 vols. Boston, Little, 1900. (Vol. 1,
Jan. 13; Vol. 2, June 9.)
— Knights of the Cross. Tr. by S. A. Binion.
3 vols. N.Y., Fenno, 1900. (Vols.
1–2, Jan. 20; Vol. 3, Dec. 15.)
— Knights of the Cross. A special trans-
lation. 2 vols. N.Y., Street, 1900.
(Vol. 1, Apr. 21; Vol. 2, Oct. 6.)
— Knights of the Cross. Tr. by B. Dahl.
N.Y., Ogilvie, Dec. 22, 1900. [Abridged.]
Warsaw.

1906, July.   Na Polu Chwały. Warsaw.
— On the Field of Glory. Tr. by J. Curtin.
Boston, Little, Feb. 3, 1906.
— The Field of Glory. Tr. by Henry Britoff.
N.Y., Ogilvie, Apr. 14, 1906.
— Field of Glory. London, Lane, July 21,
1906.

In addition to the novels listed above, his tales and stories
(*Pisma*) have been collected and published in 41 vols. (Warsaw, 1880–1902.) The following English translations have
been published: —

Yanko the Musician, and other Stories. Tr. by J. Curtin.
Boston, Little, Oct. 21, 1893. (*Contents:* Yanko the
Musician. The Light-house Keeper of Aspinwall.
From the Diary of a Tutor in Poznan. Comedy of Errors:
a Sketch of American Life. Bartek the Victor.)
Lillian Morris, and other Stories. Tr. by J. Curtin. Boston,
Little, Oct. 27, 1894. (*Contents:* Lillian Morris. Sachem.
Yamyol. The Bull-Fight.)

Let us follow Him, and other Stories. Tr. by Vatslaf A.
Hlasko and Thos. H. Bullick. N.Y., Fenno [copyrighted,
1897]. (*Contents:* Let us follow Him. Sielanka. Be
Blessed. Light in Darkness. Orso. Memories of Mari-
posa.)

Hania. Tr. by J. Curtin. Boston, Little, Dec. 11, 1897.
(*Contents:* Prologue to Hania: The Old Servant.
Hania. Tartar Captivity. Let us follow Him. Be thou
Blessed. At the Source. Charcoal Sketches. The Or-
ganist of Ponikla. Lux in Tenebris Lucet. On the
Bright Shore. That Third Woman.)

So runs the World. Tr. by S. C. de Soissons. London and
N.Y., Neely, Mar. 19, 1898. (*Contents:* Henryk Sienkiewicz. Zola. Whose Fault? The Verdict. Win or Lose.)

Sielanka, and other stories. From the Polish by J. Curtin.
Boston, Little, Oct. 29, 1898. (*Contents:* Sielanka:
a Forest Picture. For Bread. Orso. Whose Fault?
The Decision of Zeus. On a Single Card. Yanko the
Musician. Bartek the Victor. Across the Plains.
From the Diary of a Tutor in Poznan. The Light-house
Keeper of Aspinwall. Yamyol. The Bull-Fight. Sa-
chem. A Comedy of Errors. A Journey to Athens.
Zola.)

Let us Follow Him, and other Stories. Tr. by S. C. Slupski
and I. Young. Phila., Altemus [copyrighted, Oct. 24,
1898]. (*Contents:* Let us follow Him. Be Blessed.
Bartek the Conqueror.)

For Daily Bread, and other Stories. Tr. by Iza Young.
Phila., Altemus [1898]. (*Contents:* For Daily Bread.
An Artist's End. A Comedy of Errors.)

Tales from Sienkiewicz. Tr. by S. C. de Soissons. London,
Allen, Dec. 23, 1899. (*Contents:* A Country Artist.
In Bohemia. A Circus Hercules. The Decision of
Zeus. Anthea. Be Blessed! Whose Fault? True to
his Art. The Duel.)

Life and Death, and other Legends and Stories. Tr. by J.
Curtin. Boston, Little, Apr. 16, 1904. (*Contents:*
Life and Death: a Hindu Legend. Is He the Dearest
One? A Legend of the Sea. The Cranes. The Judg
ment of Peter and Paul on Olympus.)

The following stories have been published separately in
English: —

Let us follow Him. Tr. by J. Curtin. Boston, Little, Dec.
11, 1897.

After Bread. Tr. by Vatslaf A. Hlasko and Thos. H. Bullick.
N.Y., Fenno, June 18, 1898.

— Peasants in Exile (For Daily Bread). From the Polish by
C. O'Conor-Eccles. Notre Dame, Ind., The Ave
Maria [1898].

In the New Promised Land. Tr. by S. C. de Soissons.
London, Jarrold, 1900.

On the Sunny Shore. Tr. by S. C. de Soissons. N.Y., Fenno.
[1897].

— On the Bright Shore. From the Polish by J. Curtin.
Boston, Little, June 18, 1898.

— On the Bright Shore. To which is added, That Third
Woman. From the Polish by J. Curtin. Boston, Little,
1898.

In Vain. Tr. by J. Curtin. Boston, Little, June 17, 1899.

The Third Woman. Tr. by Nathan M. Babad. N.Y.,
Ogilvie, Apr. 23, 1898.

The Fate of a Soldier. Tr. by J. C. Bay. N.Y., Ogilvie
[copyrighted, Sept. 3, 1898].

— The New Soldier. N.Y., Hurst.

Hania. Tr. by Vatslaf A. Hlasco and Thos. H. Bullick.
N.Y., Fenno.

In Monte Carlo. Tr. by S. C. de Soissons. London, Greening,
Sept. 16, 1899.

The Judgment of Peter and Paul on Olympus. To which is
added: Be thou Blessed. Tr. by J. Curtin. Boston,
Little, Nov. 3, 1900.
Dust and Ashes. N.Y., Hurst.
Her Tragic Fate. N.Y., Hurst.
Where Worlds Meet. N.Y., Hurst.

ROBERT LOUIS STEVENSON
13 November 1850–3 December 1894

1866.	The Pentland Rising: a Page of History, 1666. Pp. 22. Edinburgh, Elliot.
1868.	The Charity Bazaar: an allegorical Dialogue. Pp. 4. 4°. Edinburgh. (Privately Printed.)
1871.	Notice of a New Form of Intermittent Light for Lighthouses. (From the Transactions of the Royal Scottish Society of Arts, Vol. 8, 1870–1871.) Edinburgh, Neill.
1873.	The Thermal Influence of Forests. (From the Proceedings of the Royal Society of Edinburgh.) Edinburgh, Neill.
1875.	An Appeal to the Clergy of the Church of Scotland. Edinburgh, Blackwood.
1878, May 16.	An Inland Voyage. London, Kegan Paul.
Dec. 18.	Edinburgh. Picturesque Notes. London, Seeley, 1879 [1878]. (*Portfolio.*)
1879, June 17.	Travels with a Donkey in the Cevennes. London, Kegan Paul.
1880.	Deacon Brodie; or, The Double Life: a Melodrama founded on Facts. By W. E. Henley and R. L. Stevenson. (Privately Printed.)
1881, Apr. 16.	Virginibus Puerisque, and other Papers. London, Kegan Paul.

Not I, and other Poems. Pp. 8. Davos, Osbourne.

1882. Moral Emblems: a second collection of Cuts and Verses. Davos, Osbourne.

The Story of a Lie. Pp. 80. Haley and Jackson. (Suppressed.)

Mar. 15. Familiar Studies of Men and Books. London, Chatto.

Aug. 1. New Arabian Nights. 2 vols. London, Chatto.

1883, Dec. 6. Treasure Island. London, Cassell.

The Silverado Squatters. London, Chatto. (*Century Magazine*, Nov.–Dec., 1883.)

1884. Admiral Guinea. By W. E. Henley and R. L. Stevenson. Edinburgh, Clark. (Printed for Private Circulation.)

Beau Austin. By W. E. Henley and R. L. Stevenson. (Printed for Private Circulation.)

1885, Apr. 1. A Child's Garden of Verses. London, Longmans.

May 15. More New Arabian Nights. The Dynamiter. By R. L. Stevenson and Fanny Van de Grift Stevenson. London, Longmans.

Nov. 16. Prince Otto: a Romance. London, Chatto. (*Longman's Magazine*, Apr.–Oct., 1885.) Macaire. By W. E. Henley and R. L. Stevenson. (Printed for Private Circulation.)

1886, Jan. 15. The Strange Case of Dr. Jekyll and Mr. Hyde. London, Longmans.

Aug. 2. Kidnapped: being Memoirs of the Adventures of David Balfour in the year 1751. London, Cassell.

	Some College Memories. **Edinburgh.** (30 copies Privately Printed.)
1887, Feb. 15.	The Merry Men, and other Tales and Fables. London, Chatto.
Sept. 1.	Underwoods. London, Chatto.
Dec. 6.	Memories and Portraits. London, Chatto.
	Ticonderoga. Edinburgh, Clark. (50 copies printed for the author.)
	Thomas Stevenson, Civil Engineer. (For Private Distribution.)
1888, Jan. 16.	Memoir of Fleeming Jenkin. (Prefixed to Papers of Fleeming Jenkin.) London, Longmans.
Aug. 15.	The Black Arrow: a Tale of the Two Roses. London, Cassell. (*Young Folks.*)
1889, July 1.	The Wrong Box. By R. L. Stevenson and Lloyd Osbourne. London, Longmans.
Sept. 16.	The Master of Ballantrae: a Winter's Tale. London, Cassell. (*Scribner's Magazine*, Nov., 1888–Oct., 1889.)
1890, Mar.	Father Damien: an open Letter to the Reverend Dr. Hyde of Honolulu. Pp. 32. Sydney. (Privately Printed Edition of 25 copies.)
	The South Seas. (Privately Printed.)
	Ballads. London, Chatto. (Large paper; 190 copies.)
1892, April 16.	Across the Plains; with other Memories and Essays. London, Chatto.
July 9.	The Wrecker. By R. L. Stevenson and Lloyd Osbourne. London, Cassell. (*Scribner's Magazine*, Aug., 1891–July, 1892.)
Aug. 20.	The Beach of Falesa, and The Bottle Imp. London, Cassell.

Aug. 27.	A Footnote to History: Eight Years of Trouble in Samoa. London, Cassell.
Dec. 17.	Three Plays. Deacon Brodie. Beau Austin. Admiral Guinea. By W. E. Henley and R. L. Stevenson. London, Nutt.
	An Object of Pity, or the Man Haggard. Imprinted at Amsterdam. [1892.] (For Private Distribution.)
1893, Apr. 15.	Island Nights' Entertainments. London, Cassell.
Sept. 9.	Catriona: a Sequel to "Kidnapped." London, Cassell.
Sept.	War in Samoa. Reprinted from the *Pall Mall Gazette.*
1894, Sept. 22.	The Ebb-Tide: a Trio and a Quartette. By R. L. Stevenson and Lloyd Osbourne. London, Heinemann. (*McClure's Magazine*, Feb.–July, 1894.)
Nov. 10.	The Suicide Club and The Rajah's Diamond. London, Chatto.
1895, Mar. 2.	The Amateur Emigrant from the Clyde to Sandy Hook. Chicago, Stone & Kimball.
Nov. 9.	Vailima Letters. Being Correspondence addressed by R. L. Stevenson to Sidney Colvin, Nov., 1890–Oct., 1894. London, Methuen.
1896, May 23.	Weir of Hermiston: an unfinished Romance. London, Chatto.
Sept. 5.	Songs of Travel, and other Verses. London, Chatto.
	Familiar Epistles in Verse and Prose. Pp. 18. (Printed for Private Distribution.)

288

	A Mountain Town in France: a Fragment. Pp. 20. London, Lane.
1897, Oct. 9.	St. Ives: being the Adventures of a French Prisoner in England. London, Heinemann, 1898 [1897].
1898, Feb. 26.	Macaire: a melodramatic Farce. By W. E. Henley and R. L. Stevenson. London, Heinemann.
Apr. 16.	A Lowden Sabbath Morn. London, Chatto.
	Æs Triplex. Printed for the American Subscribers to the Stevenson Memorial.
1899, Nov. 18.	Letters to his Family and Friends, selected and edited by Sidney Colvin. 2 vols. London, Methuen.
1900, Dec. 22.	In the South Seas: Account of Experiences and Observations in the Marquesas, Paumotus, and Gilbert Islands during two cruises on the Yacht "Casco," 1888, and the Schooner "Equator," 1889. London, Chatto.

HERMANN SUDERMANN
30 September 1857–

1886.	Im Zwielicht: Zwanglose Geschichten. Berlin.
1887, Feb. 10.	Frau Sorge: Roman. Berlin.
	— Dame Care. Tr. by Bertha Overbeck. London, Osgood, 1891; N.Y., Harper, 1891.
1888, Jan. 19.	Geschwister: Zwei Novellen. Berlin.
	— The Wish: a Novel. Tr. by Lily Henkel. London, Unwin, Nov. 3, 1894.
1890, Jan. 9.	Der Katzensteg: Roman. Berlin.

	— Regine. From the German by H. E. Miller. Chicago, Weeks, 1894.
	— Regina; or, The Sins of the Fathers. Tr. by Beatrice Marshall. London and N.Y., Lane, 1898.
	Die Ehre: Schauspiel. Berlin.
1891, Mar. 26.	Sodoms Ende: Drama. Berlin.
1892, June 2.	Iolanthes Hochzeit: Erzählung. Stuttgart.
1893, Mar. 23.	Heimat: Schauspiel. Stuttgart.
	— Magda. Tr. by C. E. A. Winslow. Boston, Lamson, 1896.
1894, Dec. 6.	Es war: Roman. Stuttgart.
	— The Undying Past. Tr. by Beatrice Marshall. London, N.Y., Lane, 1906.
1895, June 27.	Die Schmetterlingschlacht: Komödie. Stuttgart.
1896, Apr. 30.	Das Glück im Winkel: Schauspiel. Stuttgart.
Dec. 3.	Morituri: Teja, Fritzchen, Das Ewigmännliche. Stuttgart.
	— Teias. Tr. by Mary Harned. (*Poet-Lore*, July–Sept., 1897.)
1898, Jan. 27.	Johannes: Tragödie. Stuttgart.
	— Johannes. Tr. by W. H. Harned and Mary Harned. (*Poet-Lore*, Apr.–June, 1899.)
	— John the Baptist. Tr. by Beatrice Marshall. London, N.Y., Lane, 1909 [1908].
1899, Feb. 9.	Die drei Reiherfedern: ein dramatisches Gedicht. Stuttgart.
	— Three Heron's Feathers. Tr. by H. T. Porter. (*Poet-Lore*, Apr.–June, 1900.)
1900, May 23.	Drei Reden. Pp. 47. Stuttgart.
Oct. 25.	Johannisfeuer: Schauspiel. Stuttgart.
	— Fires of St. John. Tr. by Charlotte

Porter and H. C. Porter. (*Poet-Lore,* Jan.–Mar., 1904.)

— Fires of St. John. Tr. and adapted by Charles Swickard. Boston, Luce, Nov. 19, 1904.

— St. John's Fire. Tr. by Grace E. Polk. Minneapolis, Wilson, June 17, 1905.

1902, Feb. 27. Es lebe das Leben: Drama. Stuttgart.

— The Joy of Living. Tr. by Edith Wharton. N.Y., Scribner, Nov. 8, 1902.

Dec. 25. Verrohung in der Theaterkritik: Zeitgemässe Betrachtungen. Stuttgart.

1903, Oct. 22. Der Sturmgeselle Sokrates: Komödie. Stuttgart.

Nov. 12. Die Sturmgesellen: Ein Wort zur Abwehr. Pp. 27. Berlin.

1905, Oct. 19. Stein unter Steinen: Schauspiel. Stuttgart.

Nov. 16. Das Blumenboot: Schauspiel. Stuttgart.

1907, Oct. 24. Rosen: Vier Einakter. Stuttgart.

— Roses. Tr. by Grace Frank. N.Y., Scribner, Oct. 9, 1909.

1908, Dec. 3. Das hohe Lied: Roman. Stuttgart.

— The Song of Songs. Tr. by Thomas Seltzer. N.Y., Huebsch, Dec., 1909.

MRS. HUMPHRY WARD

(Mary Augusta Arnold)
11 June 1851–

1881, Dec. 17. Milly and Olly; or, A Holiday among the Mountains. London, Macmillan.

1884, Dec. 15. Miss Bretherton. London, Macmillan.

1885, Dec. 31. Amiel's Journal Intime, translated by Mrs. Humphry Ward. 2 vols. London, Macmillan.

1888, Mar. 1.   Robert Elsmere. 3 vols. London, Smith, Elder.

1891, Mar. 14.   University Hall: Opening Address. Pp. 45. London, Smith, Elder.

1892, Jan. 23.   The History of David Grieve. 3 vols. London, Smith, Elder.

1894, Apr. 7.   Marcella. 3 vols. London, Smith, Elder.

Aug. 4.   Unitarians and the Future: the Essex Hall Lecture, 1894. Pp. 72. London, Green.

1895, July 6.   The Story of Bessie Costrell. London, Smith, Elder. (*Cornhill Magazine,* May–July, 1895; *Scribner's Magazine,* May–July, 1895.)

1896, Oct. 3.   Sir George Tressady. London, Smith, Elder. (*Century Magazine,* Nov., 1895–Oct. 1896.)

1898, June 11.   Helbeck of Bannisdale. London, Smith, Elder.

1900, Nov. 10.   Eleanor. London, Smith, Elder. (*Harper's Magazine,* Jan.–Dec., 1900.)

1903, Mar. 21.   Lady Rose's Daughter. London, Smith, Elder. (*Harper's Magazine,* May, 1902–Apr., 1903.)

1905, Mar. 18.   The Marriage of William Ashe. London, Smith, Elder. (*Harper's Magazine,* June, 1904–May, 1905.)

1906, Mar. 3.   Play-Time of the Poor. Reprinted from the *Times.* London, Smith, Elder.

May 12.   Fenwick's Career. London, Smith, Elder.

1907, Apr. 27.   William Thomas Arnold, Journalist and Historian, by Mrs. Humphry Ward and C. E. Montague. Manchester, Sherratt. (Originally published on Feb. 23 as preface to W. T. Arnold's Fragmentary Studies on Roman Imperialism.)

LIST OF PUBLICATIONS

1908, Sept. 19.   Diana Mallory. London, Smith, Elder
                   (The Testing of Diana Mallory, *Har-
                   per's Magazine*, Nov., 1907–Oct., 1908.)
1909, May 29.   Daphne; or, Marriage à la Mode. Lon-
                   don, Cassell. (N.Y., Doubleday, June
                   5, under title "Marriage à la Mode."
                   (*McClure's Magazine*, Jan.–June, 1909.)

Printed in the United States of America.